CLAUDE DEBUSSY'S
Clair de Lune

CLAUDE DEBUSSY'S
Clair de Lune

GURMINDER KAUR
BHOGAL

OXFORD
UNIVERSITY PRESS

OXFORD
UNIVERSITY PRESS

Oxford University Press is a department of the University of Oxford. It furthers
the University's objective of excellence in research, scholarship, and education
by publishing worldwide. Oxford is a registered trade mark of Oxford University
Press in the UK and certain other countries.

Published in the United States of America by Oxford University Press
198 Madison Avenue, New York, NY 10016, United States of America.

© Oxford University Press 2018

Library of Congress Cataloging-in-Publication Data
Names: Bhogal, Gurminder Kaur, author.
Title: Claude Debussy's Clair de lune / Gurminder Kaur Bhogal.
Description: New York, NY : Oxford University Press, [2018] |
Series: Oxford keynotes | Includes bibliographical references and index.
Identifiers: LCCN 2017053469 | ISBN 9780190696061 (hardcover : alk. paper) |
ISBN 9780190696078 (pbk. : alk. paper)
Subjects: LCSH: Debussy, Claude, 1862–1918. Suite bergamasque. Clair de lune.
| Moon—Songs and music—History and criticism.
Classification: LCC ML410.D28 B5 2018 | DDC 786.2/1858—dc23
LC record available at https://lccn.loc.gov/2017053469

1 3 5 7 9 8 6 4 2

Paperback printed by WebCom, Inc., Canada
Hardback printed by Bridgeport National Bindery, Inc., United States of America

For Vir Singh Mehta and Armaan Singh Mehta

Series Editor's
INTRODUCTION

OXFORD KEYNOTES REIMAGINES THE canons of Western music for the twenty-first century. With each of its volumes dedicated to a single composition or album, the series provides an informed, critical, and provocative companion to music as artwork and experience. Books in the series explore how works of music have engaged listeners, performers, artists, and others through history and in the present. They illuminate the roles of musicians and musics in shaping Western cultures and societies, and they seek to spark discussion of ongoing transitions in contemporary musical landscapes. Each approaches its key work in a unique way, tailored to the distinct opportunities that the work presents. Targeted at performers, curious listeners, and advanced undergraduates, volumes in the series are written by expert and engaging voices in their fields, and will therefore be of significant interest to scholars and critics as well.

In selecting titles for the series, Oxford Keynotes balances two ways of defining the canons of Western music: as lists of works that critics and scholars deem to have articulated key moments in the history of the art, and as lists of works that comprise the bulk of what consumers listen to, purchase, and perform today. Often, the two lists intersect, but the overlap is imperfect. While not neglecting the first, Oxford Keynotes gives considerable weight to the second. It confronts the musicological canon with the living repertoire of performance and recording in classical, popular, jazz, and other idioms. And it seeks to expand that living repertoire through the latest musicological research.

Kevin C. Karnes
Emory University

CONTENTS

ABOUT THE
COMPANION WEBSITE

OXFORD UNIVERSITY PRESS HAS created a password-protected website to accompany *Claude Debussy's Clair de Lune*. Material that cannot be made available in the book is provided here, namely, a complete recording of Clair de Lune in its version for piano as performed by Benno Moiseiwitsch (1918) and a score of Clair de Lune. The reader is encouraged to consult these resources whenever the work is discussed in the main text. To help the reader navigate the piece, I will here indicate the different sections in relation to Moiseiwitsch's recording: the *tempo rubato* begins at 0.53, *un poco mosso* at 1.35, *en animant* at 2.04, *calmato* at 2.18, *a Tempo* at 2.41, and *morendo jusqu'à le fin* at 3.41.

Also available on the website is Verlaine's poem "Clair de Lune" in French and English (my translation). All translations are mine unless otherwise indicated. Where possible, color reproductions of images contained in the book are shown. Links to online material such as YouTube videos and blogs can also be found here. Online resources are indicated in the text with Oxford's symbol ⊙.

www.oup.com/us/cdcdl
Username: Music5
Password: Book1745

The reader is invited to explore the full catalog of Oxford Keynotes volumes on the series homepage.
www.oup.com/us/oxfordkeynotes

ACKNOWLEDGMENTS

I T IS IMMENSELY SATISFYING to commemorate the centenary of the death of Claude Debussy with a book dedicated to the discussion of his well-known piece Clair de Lune. For this opportunity, I would like to thank Kevin Karnes, series editor, and Suzanne Ryan, editor, both of whom have been supportive and welcoming throughout the process of conducting research and writing. I am particularly grateful to Kevin for indulging my interest to write on this topic, not to mention his superb editorial skills and willingness to advise along the way. Also to be thanked are the anonymous readers of the book proposal and manuscript; I appreciate their engagement with the ideas presented here and excellent suggestions for improvement. I am humbled to have had the support of esteemed scholars of French music during the research phase. My warmest appreciation goes to Jonathan Dunsby, Annegret Fauser, Peter Kaminsky, François de Médici, and Richard Langham Smith.

My home institution, Wellesley College, has provided support on many levels. For their contributions, I am grateful to the students who participated in my seminar Finding France in French Piano Music. Related to this course, the Music Department helped organize a week-long residency that featured Dr. Roy Howat as our guest artist. We learned a great deal from Roy's masterful tour of French piano music and from his idiosyncratic approach to examining issues of style, aesthetics, performance, and editorial practice. Roy's generosity extended to a close reading of this manuscript, for which I am extremely grateful. Tamar Barzel and Kariann Goldschmitt also deserve special thanks for their valuable feedback on my analysis of Debussy's piece in popular culture. In addition, I extend my warm gratitude to faculty and staff of the Music and French Departments who supported the residency, Carol Lubkowski for offering assistance through the music library, Pallas Catenella for making musical examples, Ju Young Kwag for her help with research, and Tyler Duerson for saving me on technical fronts many a time.

I enjoyed compiling the rich array of audio and visual material presented here. For access to the earliest audio recordings of Clair de Lune, I would like to thank Donald Manildi of the International Piano Archives, University of Maryland, and Daniel Barolsky. Daniel is also to be thanked for alerting me to Slim Gaillard's wonderful rendition of Clair de Lune. Richard Masters responded generously to my inquiries regarding George Copeland. I thank Rick for sharing recordings, primary sources, and his own invaluable research with me. My gratitude also extends to the Victoria and Albert Museum, the New York Public Library, Houghton Library at Harvard University, and the Morgan Library and Museum for supplying special images. I am grateful to the Weisgard family for allowing me to use an illustration from Leonard Weisgard's book *Look at the Moon* for my front cover.

The love and support of my family has ensured the completion of this book. I am deeply indebted to my parents and parents-in-law, Mridul, my siblings, and my nieces and nephews. This book is dedicated with love to my sons, Vir and Armaan.

CLAUDE DEBUSSY'S
Clair de Lune

CHAPTER 1

YOUR CLAIR DE LUNE

> I only know two pieces: One is 'Clair de Lune,' and the
> other one isn't.
>
> Victor Borge

O N CLAUDE DEBUSSY'S 151ST birthday (August 22, 2013), the French composer was bestowed with what some might see as a great honor of the digital era, a Google doodle. Clair de Lune was selected by Leon Hong, a "doodler," as the sonic backdrop for an animation that depicts a Paris-like city at night.[1] In the doodle, Debussy's piano piece evokes an imaginary landscape wherein a play button releases balloons into a moonlit sky to reveal a motor car, a unicyclist, and a barge making their way through the city. Viewers will notice how the rhythm of flickering lights corresponds with the placement of melodic gestures, much as the billows of smoke that escape from chimney tops coincide with moments marking the ends of musical phrases. Gathering clouds create an opportunity for romance: serendipitously, they burst into a shower of rain just as a man and a woman cross paths in their boats, the woman offering the man shelter under her bright red umbrella (figure 1.1). (Listen to audio example 1.1 ▶.)

While this doodle appeals to our penchant for things elegant and French—Hong said his goal was "to make a doodle that would look nice as a French wine label"—it also illustrates one reason why Clair de Lune is highly popular today: this music sits just as comfortably in the background as in the foreground of our listening experiences, and often at the same time. This might sound like a confusing state—and one from which a listener might want to extricate herself—but this is not so. Clair de Lune does not hold its listener hostage, ensuring that every note is heard. As seen here, the combination of music and image is especially effective, since there is no sense of competition between them. Sonic and visual dimensions cultivate a fluid relationship as they come in and out of auditory and visual focus, sometimes overlapping, sometimes not.

Similarly, Debussy idealized a flexible approach toward hearing music, one that invited his audiences to let their

FIGURE 1.1   Google Doodle for Claude Debussy's 151st Birthday.

imaginations roam as they listened, guided by his work. Debussy wrote to his friend the composer Paul Dukas in 1901: "It would be enough if they [audience members] could no longer recognize their own grey, dull faces, if they felt that for a moment they had been dreaming of an imaginary country, that's to say one that can't be found on the map."[2] According to Debussy, the most expressive music bears the potential to help listeners escape the mundane realities of their existence. But what makes his music successful in this regard? What is it about the alluring soundscape of Clair de Lune that helps us lose our sense of self as we become immersed in thoughts of places and things that don't exist?

While these kinds of questions motivate my study of how listeners engage with Clair de Lune, I am also eager to explore the ramifications of a comment made by George Copeland, an American pianist who studied with the composer and who served as an ambassador for Debussy's music in the United States from 1904 until 1964: "It is necessary to abandon yourself completely and let the music do as it will with you."[3] This goal is suggested in the frequency with which musicians emphasize temporal fluidity in the opening measures; in many performances the delicate placement of each gesture punctuates musical time in a seemingly improvisatory way, allowing us to gradually lose awareness of our surroundings as we are drawn toward the sparse yet mesmerizing utterances of the opening phrases, unable to predict what might come next. The drawn-out gaps between each musical event of the melody remind us of Debussy's privileging of silence. Debussy described his use of silence in the opera *Pelléas et Mélisande* (1902) in terms of its beauty and potential for expression; Debussy told the poet Pierre Louÿs in 1895, "Silence is a beautiful thing. . . . The empty bars in *Pelléas* are evidence of my love of this sort of emotional expression."[4] While later avant-garde composers like the American John Cage took their lead from such French artists as Debussy and Erik Satie, Debussy's cryptic remarks are less an invitation to listen closely to the music that envelops us than they are a direction to do the opposite—that is, to withdraw from listening too closely, thereby allowing music to transport us to a realm where each listener is free to contemplate the piece's sonorous beauty and expressive significance for herself. This is one reason why Clair de Lune continues to inspire today: as long as human beings are free to interpret and create, Debussy's composition will always be reimagined in new ways, across new contexts and through diverse media, as performers and audiences mull over their personal connections with this piece. From their distinct standpoints, the five chapters of this book work toward explaining why Clair de Lune is just *that* kind of piece.

It is with ideas of reinterpretation and flexible listening in mind that the next chapter will consider how Clair de Lune moves within the pathways of popular culture. We will see how Debussy's piece serves as the perfect accompaniment to *something else*, be it a movie, a commercial, a video game, or an animation. Although this music is subtle enough to fade into the background, Clair de Lune's expressive intensity ensures that its presence is always known and felt. In thinking about how Debussy evokes atmosphere in music—the primary quality to which visual artists are drawn—I give special attention to how aspects of timbre, sonority, texture, and figuration appeal to our senses. This chapter will also consider reinterpretations of the work across a range of popular music idioms, where a tendency toward abstraction reveals how Debussy's piece functions as a muse for intertextual experimentation.

Chapter 3 will contextualize Clair de Lune in relation to the *Suite Bergamasque*, a collection of four pieces of which it is the third: Prélude, Menuet, Clair de Lune, and Passepied. This brief chapter will trace the long and somewhat complicated history of the suite, which was begun in 1890 but completed and published much later, in 1905. A consideration of the historical background allows us to glimpse Debussy's idiosyncratic approach to composition. Moreover, it is only when viewing Clair de Lune in relation to its siblings in the set that we can begin to appreciate the significance of the stylistic and aesthetic ways in which it stands as the odd one out. The chapter will also explore the numerous meanings of the term *bergamasque*, the most alluring of which is a reference to Paul Verlaine's "Clair de Lune," the poem that opens his collection of poetry from 1869, *Fêtes galantes*.

Following Debussy's cue, chapter 4 will use Verlaine's poem as a springboard for exploring connections between music and poetry. My point of departure is not Verlaine but the eighteenth-century painter Jean-Antoine Watteau, whose *fêtes galantes* scenes of aristocrats at play infuse both Verlaine's poem and Debussy's piece. Nineteenth-century writers and artists were especially drawn to the recurring figure of Pierrot in Watteau's decorative landscapes, and Pierrot was well known within France, having been brought over in the early eighteenth century as a stock character by traveling Italian comedy troupes who performed the theatrical forms of the commedia dell'arte. When Watteau's work was revived by artists and writers in the early nineteenth century, it took only a few creative and conceptual maneuvers for Pierrot's shimmery appearance and persistent solitude to stand in for the image of the moon. A consideration of Debussy's early song settings of Verlaine's "Clair de Lune" from 1882 and 1891 will preface a closer study of Clair de Lune in its version for piano. The subtle pianism of the piece draws attention to issues of performance and interpretation, which I examine in relation to its earliest recordings.

Chapter 5 will broaden our perspective to consider visual and literary portrayals of the moon that likely shaped Debussy's conception in his Clair de Lune. In situating his composition alongside the work of late-nineteenth-century writers and artists, this closing chapter will loop back to the opening, to perform the important task of contextualizing how the moon came to be associated with themes of dreaming, romance, melancholy, and such in the Western imagination. The wide range of nocturnal scenes explored in the chapter call our attention to Debussy's treatment of a subject that was then in vogue and encouraged constant experimentation, as seen in the varied treatment of the moon as it passed through the hands of the Romantics to the Symbolists. This chapter will also examine some of Debussy's other nocturnal-themed compositions. In the end, Debussy's nostalgia for Watteau, as seen in his final letters and writings, reveals which moon was, for him, the fairest of them all.

The kind of artistic border crossing undertaken by Clair de Lune as it moves within the realm of classical music and beyond has inspired discussion of issues pertaining to the categories of high and low art, influence and intertextuality, and registral play between popular and classical expressive gestures.[5] My experience of working with digital media as I was writing this book offers additional insights on the problem of how to assess the enormous success of Clair de Lune as it mediates classical and popular realms. In one respect, the "shuffle" function in an app like iTunes creates a potentially egalitarian system of organization, where proximity between different genres of music suggests stylistic equality. While the content of a user's music library predetermines the level of diversity, social media platforms such as Facebook and YouTube go one step further in offering an open forum where anyone, regardless of their level of musical training or expertise, can contribute to—and feel empowered as a participant in—conversations about music. By destabilizing the high-art/low-art binary in these ways, digital technology makes gestures toward inclusiveness by opening up spaces where listeners from all over the world can feel comfortable sharing their innermost thoughts, as elicited by a piece of music, with a virtual cohort of complete strangers.

Opportunities such as these are socially significant given their potential to create a level playing field where fans of varying backgrounds and sensibilities can gather online to engage in dialogue about a favorite piece of music. In these environments, questions of influence are rarely organized along an Oedipal trajectory where a dominant source must be overcome. I would argue that the most significant impact of digital technology as it pertains to our understanding of Clair de Lune can be perceived in how the work's migration across contexts opens up an appreciation for multiple authorships, as creative interpreters are presented as working alongside each other in a utopian space of never-ending renewal and intertextual richness.

Another reason for the seemingly universal appeal of Clair de Lune has to do with the abstract concept of nothingness, one that brings together the diverse intellectual traditions of philosophers and physicists as they mull over existential issues of being and nonbeing, presence and absence. In one regard, the modest Clair de Lune is brimful with meaning as conveyed through the multiple levels on which this piece speaks to its listeners from that of the programmatic, as prompted by the narrative of moonlight, to the technical, as understood through the understated complexity and refined nuances of Debussy's musical language. Seen in this way, this piece could be heard as combining creativity with logic, and one could quite easily stop at this point, feeling considerably satisfied in having reached the conclusion that Clair de Lune is a piece in which the composer explores the topic of the moon through a specific array of musical techniques. To do so, however, would do an injustice to Debussy's subtle poetics, wherein the primary goal of music is to evoke beauty and mystery. As he wrote in a letter to André Poniatowski in 1893: "Music . . . is a dream from which the veils have been lifted. It's not even the expression of a feeling, it's the feeling itself."[6]

For Debussy, it was nothing short of a crime to claim precise meaning for his music, that is, to argue that his music *represents* something. He made this viewpoint amply clear in his response to the critic Pierre Lalo, who complained with regard to Debussy's purported efforts to evoke the sea in *La Mer*, "I do not hear, I do not see, I do not smell the sea."[7] Debussy's deliberate avoidance of this kind of musical artificiality is key to understanding his aesthetics, a point made perfectly by the pianist Alfred Cortot. While Debussy's programmatic titles suggest atmosphere, Cortot maintained that such titles are "elastic enough not to freeze the interpretation by a puerile care for imitation yet at the same time definite enough to maintain it in the quality of expression required by them."[8] Even as the topic of moonlight infuses the music with a certain atmosphere, Cortot seems to say, it is essential that the moon does not in the end limit our experience of the music. The scholar Peter Dayan sees a correlate for Debussy's aesthetic preferences in the literary goals of French writers such as Gustave Flaubert, who sought to write a book about nothing, and Stéphane Mallarmé, for whom beauty was irreconcilable with meaning.[9] While French poets like Paul Verlaine praised the imprecision of music's ability to say something—Verlaine opened his poem of 1874 "Art poétique" with the phrase "Music before all else"—Debussy was drawn to the same quality of ephemerality as inspired by the mystery of nature. "Music is a mysterious mathematical process whose elements are a part of infinity," he wrote. "It is allied to the movement of the waters, to the play of curves described by changing breezes."[10]

This brief meditation on how a piece like Clair de Lune invites interpretation in the same moment that it resists the assignment of meaning might seem like a futile way of opening an inquiry into Debussy's music. Even as I foreground the philosophical nuances of Debussy's thinking in preparation for my exploration of his thought and practice, my main motivation is to offer a preliminary reason for why this piece has achieved widespread appeal. The moon is an age-old object whose light touches each of us; Debussy's unwillingness to speak of the multiple moons that filter through the shadows of his own inspiration— whether those of Watteau or Verlaine, J. M. W. Turner or Charles Baudelaire—overlays his composition with nocturnal images and sensations the sheer range of which offer the listener multiple ways to craft a connection with a piece that feels wholly unique. Unlike the sun, whose raging energy repels the eye, the moon invites us to gaze at its blank, changing face, calling us to reveal our innermost dreams and anxieties as we trace familiar shapes and images on its distant surface. In advising against the analysis of his music, Debussy maintained: "The beauty of a work of art is something that will always remain mysterious; that is to say one can never find out exactly 'how it is done.'"[11] What remains mysterious and deceptive in Clair de Lune is how this modest composition makes each of us feel as though it was written especially—just—for us.

CHAPTER 2

RESONANCES OF CLAIR DE LUNE

D EBUSSY'S CLAIR DE LUNE turns up frequently in un-expected places. Pop songs, TV shows, commercials, movies, and video games have incorporated this piece in unusual and creative ways. Why does mainstream media turn to this work so often? What is it about Clair de Lune that continues to draw audiences and elicit personal confessions of how it brings them to tears, makes them feel sad, peaceful, joyful, spiritual? How can a piece of music do this? And why this one?

Given the high esteem in which Clair de Lune is held within popular culture, it would be satisfying to offer a history of the piece that emphasizes how hard Debussy labored over its content, working away at the evanescent themes, haunting harmonies, and translucent textures until he had perfected his work of art. Just as practical constraints of time and money often weigh heavily in the consideration of whether or not to use preexisting music in commercials, film, and video games, the underwhelming truth is that Debussy likely sketched this piece in 1890 and then rushed to finish it off for publication around March or April 1905.[1] At this time, his love affair with Emma Bardac was in full bloom and, to Debussy's detriment, common knowledge in Paris. Following his sudden disappearance to the Isle of Jersey with Emma in July 1904, his wife, Rosalie Texier, attempted suicide, and many of his closest friends turned a cold shoulder toward the composer after his return to Paris. Debussy was a bon vivant, someone who preferred to savor fine food and Japanese art than pay off his debts (of which he had many). Although he was generally irresponsible with his finances, this was a time in his life when financial security was especially important. Fortunately, his recently completed opera, *Pelléas et Mélisande*, had been hailed a success in the French press, and publishers were keen to sell his music. In 1905, Debussy gave the publishing house of Jacques Durand exclusive rights to his music, and he begrudgingly started revising old works such as the *Suite Bergamasque*, a collection of four piano pieces begun in 1890, of which Clair de Lune is the third. During this decade, Debussy also composed a number of new works, including the orchestral tone poem *La Mer* (1905) and several piano pieces. Some of these were inspired by vivid memories of Javanese and Vietnamese music he had heard at the 1889 Paris World's Fair (like *Estampes*, 1903), while others reflected his long-standing fascination with water, fairy tales, nature, and the music of Jean-Philippe Rameau, his favorite musical topics (*Pour le Piano*, 1901; *L'isle joyeuse*, 1904; *Images*, 1905 and 1907). Although these were hard years financially, they were happy ones: Debussy was living with Bardac, and the light of his life, Claude-Emma Debussy, was born to them in October 1905.

The enormous appeal of Clair de Lune poses a conundrum: given the substantial amount of piano music composed by Debussy during this decade, why did Clair de Lune gain stardom? Much of Debussy's piano music was avidly discussed in the Parisian press after being premiered by the Catalan virtuoso Ricardo Viñes. But the *Suite Bergamasque*, and Clair de Lune in particular, received little attention. While Debussy was proud of pieces like the *Images* and the *Études* (1915), he barely mentioned Clair de Lune in his correspondence and writings, an absence which seems to suggest he had little regard for it. Who could have predicted the level of fame and prestige this piece was destined to achieve within the space of a few decades?

This chapter explores how Clair de Lune has been reimagined, and continues to be reworked, in popular contexts, a task that will always remain a tad incomplete, given the speed with which new versions of this piece are constantly appearing. Drawing on a sample of musical and visual examples, I will examine how Debussy's music is used to communicate a range of emotions and moods, which intensify and prolong the overtly dreamy quality of this piece.[2] I will consider how various recompositions of the work display their creators' ingenuity, and how they have functioned in the domain of advertising, where the work's positive status as cliché and inherent stylistic flexibility have been used to endorse a diverse range of products. Finally, I will consider examples drawn from film and video games, to highlight Debussy's gift for creating a style of music that is connotative, as opposed to denotative, in its aspirations. Indeed, Debussy's extraordinary ability to cultivate mood through sound has attracted novelists, directors, and video-game designers to this piece time and again. In the end, the secret of Clair de Lune's popularity may be attributed to the myriad ways in which the title—"Moonlight"—is imagined, an observation that helps explain why this piece lends itself to frequent creative adaptation across boundaries of genre and culture.

MUSICAL REIMAGININGS

Despite his impossibly high standards, Debussy was not averse to the idea that other musicians might want to transcribe his music. In the case of Clair de Lune, André Caplet, a French composer and conductor, was probably the first to adapt this piece in his especially coloristic transcription for orchestra. Caplet shared a special relationship with Debussy. The two met in 1907; Debussy valued Caplet's musical judgment as well as his "gift of conjuring up an atmosphere."[3] From 1910 until the outbreak of the First World War, Caplet served as an ambassador for Debussy's music, conducting performances of *Pelléas et Mélisande* in Boston and London. Caplet even performed his own orchestrated version of Debussy's piano suite, *Children's Corner*, in New York in 1910.[4]

Worth noting is the significant fan base that was growing around Debussy's music on the East Coast, particularly in Boston, by the turn of the twentieth century. George Copeland paved the way with his recitals of Debussy's piano music as early as 1904. Concert reviews in American journals such as the *Musical Courier* documented other pianists following quickly in Copeland's footsteps. A reviewer of Augusta Cottlow's recital in 1908 was appreciative of Debussy's music: "This painter of subtle and illusive moods has written nothing more charming than the 'Clair de lune.'"[5] Yet there were those who were not enamored with Debussy's pianistic innovations; a prominent composer and Harvard professor, Edward Burlingame Hill, found himself regularly defending Debussy's piano music against accusations of it offering too much "rare and exotic aroma."[6]

Although it is difficult to say when exactly Clair de Lune took off in American musical life, it is clear that this piece was "in the air" during the early decades of the twentieth century across concert halls and movie theaters. The composer Walter Piston (a student of Burlingame Hill) made an orchestral arrangement in 1936, as did Leopold Stokowski in 1937 (his version was used in Walt Disney's *Fantasia*, discussed below). As we will see, Hollywood's commercialization of Clair de Lune was paralleled in the popular music industry, which brought Debussy's innovations into the folds of diverse musical idioms catering to adult musical tastes (also known as "easy listening") after World War II.[7] Clair de Lune's simple textures, slowly shifting harmonies, and undulating melodies facilitated its identification with what Pierre Bourdieu calls a "light" aesthetic, while offering unceasing opportunity for adaptation.[8] More than anything, the lush sound of Debussy's composition as conveyed through floating melodies and sustained, rippling arpeggiation was the flame to which musicians were drawn; the "soft-focus sound" associated with Debussy found a natural counterpart in the genre of mood music promoted by the "easy listening" industry after the war.[9] The following discussion highlights how Clair de Lune was reworked in popular music contexts, while keeping in sight the changing notions of taste and cultural value in relation to which Debussy's piece was reconceived.

Domenico Savino (music) and Mitchell Parish (lyrics) recast Debussy's piece in the form of a Latin-inspired big band vocal jazz ballad called "Moonlight Love" in 1956.[10] Perry Como recorded it for Victor in October 1956 and performed it when he appeared on Walter Winchell's show on NBC the same month. *Billboard* magazine described the recording as showing "the relaxed, intimate Como touch," which is certainly evident in Como's silky performance with its flexible rhythmic delivery and effortless vocal swoops.[11]

Savino's arrangement is especially creative in its use of Clair de Lune's *un poco mosso* (m. 27) as an introduction and refrain. (Listen to audio example 2.1 ▶.) The orchestration alludes to topics of otherworldliness and exoticism through familiar musical tropes: against the backdrop of shimmering violins in the introduction, the warm, prominent timbre of the French horns draws attention to the expressive flat seventh. The chorus does the same in the refrains; a common feature of popular music and film music of the time, the female wordless choir accompanies Como's melody, "I wait for you where the lilacs grow in the stillness of the night," thereby privileging a "soft-focus . . . gauzy" sound to evoke nocturnal mystery. In keeping with the cinematic origin of this term, Rebecca Leydon reminds us how such feminized sounds seem to "emanate from an indefinite location."[12] By showcasing this passage, Savino points to the modal quality of Debussy's writing as having caught his ear, inspiring him to create a sonic hook that brought—to his mind, at least—the sounds of French impressionism into contact with American popular music. The following examples continue to explore how these kinds of sonic blends participated in the articulation of a middle-class American identity in the postwar era.

A similarly sumptuous arrangement is heard in "Magic Moon," recorded by The Rays (words and music by Frank Slay and Bob Crewe). In a front-page article entitled " 'Clair de Lune' Is Pop Styled," *Billboard Music Week* notes that this song was released in 1961, although it was in fact cut earlier.[13] This doo-wop rendition takes as its rhythmic foundation the gentle triplet pulse that Debussy deliberately avoids in his opening measures. A common feature of rhythm and blues ballads, the triplets bring a nice lilt to the song, lending some stability to the call-and-response textures and an opportunity to play with rhythmic groupings as heard in the shift to a duple patterning at "leading her straight to my arms." "Magic Moon" parallels the form of Debussy's original, as heard in the rising tension of the middle section, "Oh! Answer me, answer me, if you hear my prayer," whose intensity matches that of the buildup from Debussy's *tempo rubato* (mm. 15–26). (Listen to audio example 2.2 ▶.) While this phrase fades away into soft arpeggiation in Debussy's version, Slay and Crewe recompose this passage, using the technique of rising chromaticism to highlight the lead singer's extraordinarily long sustained high note on "Magic moon above / Won't you send me someone to *love*?" The ascending chromaticism is balanced here by descent as the music moves back to the home key, in anticipation of the piano's return to the familiar thirds of Debussy's opening. The closely spaced, resonating harmonies of the singers define the genre of doo-wop while recasting the warm timbre and sonorities of Debussy's composition.

By the 1960s, Clair de Lune had become a staple of American musical life, both classical and mainstream. Alongside performances in piano recitals through the 1910s, 1920s, 1930s, and 1940s, we also see an increase in the number of arrangements for instruments like the guitar (Mario Parodi published an arrangement in 1950 with Ricordi) and violin (Jascha Heifetz recorded this piece for Decca in 1945). Celebrity classical musicians who had crossed over into the commercial sphere also played a role in familiarizing American audiences with Debussy's music. José Iturbi recorded Clair de Lune for Victor in 1945, after having played it in the film *Music for Millions* (1944); Victor Borge included it in a comedy show in July 1947; and Liberace recorded it for Columbia in 1954, going on to perform the piece on *The Dean Martin Show* in May 1966, accompanied by female dancers who swirled and twirled their chiffon gowns while he played (no doubt inspired by the choreographic innovations of Isadora Duncan, who had interpreted Debussy's music in a similar vein as early as 1915). Meanwhile, "easy listening"-style adaptations of Debussy's piece continued to evolve as heard in Steve Lawrence's bolero-styled cover of "Moonlight Love" in "My Clair de lune" (1962) (lyrics by Jerry Leiber and Mike Stoller). (Listen to audio example 2.3 ▶.)[14]

The versatile jazz musician Slim Gaillard took Borge's co-medic use of the piece one step further, opening his segment on *The Steve Allen Show* in 1962 with the introductory measures of Debussy's piece played with his hands facing palms up, much to the amusement of the audience. (Listen to audio example 2.4 ⊚.)[15] While Gaillard knew his unor-thodox style of playing would elicit laughter, his use of Clair de Lune as a basis for comedy reinforces the point that this piece was sufficiently well known to American audiences by the early sixties that he could successfully integrate it into his improvisatory musical banter using just the opening phrase. This use highlights the fact that Debussy's piece had exhausted its cultural value as "high art" by this time.

As discussed by the music theorist Matthew Brown, the sixties were a time when the exotic "tiki style" (a hybrid of Hawaiian and Western musical idioms) was in vogue. Brown explores tiki versions of Clair de Lune in Martin Denny's *A Taste of Honey* (1962) and Arthur Lyman's *Ilikai* (1967).[16] Also noteworthy is Les Baxter's rendition for Moog synthesizer (*Moog Rock*, 1968), where the rather brisk tempo offers a metric reinterpretation of Clair de Lune, which emphasizes the triplet pulse and its projec-tion of 9/8 meter.[17] As with The Rays' "Magic Moon," what is especially noteworthy about these examples is how they each reinstate a clearly articulated sense of meter. Debussy relied on metric instability to open the ears of his listeners and draw them deeper into a sonic world characterized by qualities of mystery and ambiguity. In the guise of his alter ego, Monsieur Croche—a pun on the musical value of an eighth note, a *croche* in French—Debussy wrote arti-cles complaining about uninterested audiences: "Have you noticed their almost drugged expression of boredom, indifference and even stupidity?"[18] In contrast, Les Baxter's re-composition allows audience members to stay within their comfort zones so that they can effectively sit back and chill, precisely the kind of sentiment that characterized tiki music in the first place. (Listen to audio example 2.5 ▶.)

From the 1960s to the present day, Clair de Lune has been musically reworked in many different ways, each version building on and responding to the imaginative undertakings of prior reworkings. In parallel with Hollywood, early vocal adaptations allowed a specific array of feelings and moods to coalesce around Debussy's piece. While many of these associations endure into the present, they have also been tweaked in ways that reflect contemporaneous perceptions of Debussy's musical style. For instance, interpretations of moonlight as offering an opportunity for love and romance, as heard with Perry Como and The Rays, were continued by the Chicago-based progressive rock band Styx, whose song "Clair de Lune / Ballerina," (from the album *Crystal Ball*, 1976) uses the opening section of Debussy's piece to preface a song about heartbreak and rejection in the style of a power ballad, complete with virtuosic riffs on the electric guitar. Michael Long's discussion of registral play explains how the use of classical quotation in this way functions to break an "implied contract between song and audience," since the listener is not greeted with the customary introduction at the outset of the song.[19] In "Ballerina," Clair de Lune bridges the "registers" between classical music and rock, while using its link to the topic of moonlight, and various associative cultural meanings, to shift the listener's mood toward one that is sympathetic to the sentiments of the song. In this way, an acculturated listener will already know the song is about lost love even before the singer's lyrics kick in with the line "It seems you finally had to choose / I guess there was no other way / Between my love and satin shoes / I knew the words you'd have to say." (Listen to audio example 2.6 ▶.)[20]

Meanwhile, associations of Clair de Lune with relaxation and "easy listening" continue to be exploited by the New Age industry, which often features Debussy's music on audio compilations designed with the express purpose of reducing stress and anxiety. George Melachrino was among the first to venture into this terrain with his album *Music for Reading*, where Clair de Lune is the opening track (recorded for Victor in 1958). Recently, several YouTube channels tout Debussy's piece as a form of relaxing study music, with some offering an extended duration so that it can function as pleasant background noise to which students can presumably "zone out" while they study. The endless-loop option has also been welcomed as the perfect music for aiding sleep. Especially imaginative in this regard are the multiple-hour recordings designed for babies. One such version, for synthesized music box, recalls Les Baxter's work and directs our attention to how his transcription for Moog synthesizer effectively opened up avenues for experimentation with Clair de Lune in the domain of electronic music. As explored by Brown, Isao Tomita likely responded to Baxter in his novelty version for the Moog III synthesizer, as heard on Tomita's album *Snowflakes Are Dancing* (1974). (Listen to audio example 2.7 ▶.)[21] While significantly different in their aesthetic aims, recent remixes using 8-bit technology and those by the Australian group Flight

Facilities might also be heard as participating in the same lineage. These reworkings reflect a mutual interest in using electronics to manipulate sound as a means of evoking the sense of otherworldliness heard in "Moonlight Love" and versions for Moog.

My final example in this section, "Clair de Lune," is featured on Flight Facilities' album *Down to Earth* (2014). (Listen to audio example 2.8 ⊙.) This example is especially inventive in its use of a rising D♭–F motif as the harmonic and metric basis for a song in a clear duple meter.[22] In a curious parallel with Savino, Flight Facilities also take their point of inspiration from the harmonic motion of the *un poco mosso*, which they adapt to the genre of electronica/house music while paying tribute to Debussy's preference for floating, wispy melodies. The filtered voice of Christine Hoberg gradually emerges above the repeating D♭–F pattern in a free-floating melody, while a melodic motif derived from Debussy's juxtaposition of D♭ major and F minor chords becomes increasingly prominent as the song progresses (listen closely at 1.04 and 1.54). Although techniques of layering and repetition are common in electronic pop, the textural clarity of their presentation here shows how a few nuggets derived from Debussy's composition—a chord progression, a repeating melodic figure, a descending D♭–C melodic motif—can be digitally processed to generate the expressive content of an entire song. Furthermore, the manipulation of stereo space deepens the connection between Debussy's piece and its suggestion of otherworldliness, especially at those moments where shifts in electronic timbre simulate the effect of wordless vocals.

The experiments with timbre that Baxter, Tomita, and Flight Facilities prioritize bring to our attention the multiple other instrumental palettes to which Debussy's piece has been adapted. In addition to transcriptions for guitar and violin, players of the accordion, harp, cello, flute, Theremin, pedal steel guitar, marimba, and pan flute have arranged this piece in ways that exhibit the expressive lyricism of their instruments. Following Slim Gaillard's effortless riffs on Debussy's opening motif, Clair de Lune has been taken up in other improvisatory genres: the guitarist Laurindo Almeida recorded a samba version for Capitol records in the 1970s; recently, the saxophonist Kamasi Washington released an album (*The Epic*, 2015) where Clair le Lune is conceived in a style that mixes aspects of jazz with gospel, relying once again on a wordless chorus to evoke the trope of otherworldliness. Among the most commercially widespread uses of Debussy's piece at this moment is Lana Del Ray's incorporation of a piano version at the end of her song "Freak" (*Honeymoon*, 2015). (Listen to audio example 2.9 ⊙.) Debussy's music accompanies a video of nymph-like women swimming aimlessly underwater, the dreamy quality of Debussy's piece serving to underscore the narrative of freedom and escape as foregrounded in the song: "Baby if you wanna leave, come to California, be a freak like me, too / Screw your anonymity, loving me is all you need to feel."[23] While "easy listening" renditions of the 1950 and 1960s were oriented toward adult tastes, Del Rey confers on Clair de Lune a distinctly hip vibe that resonates with a younger audience.

Whether it is used as a prelude (Styx), a postlude (Del Ray), or a sonic hook (Perry Como, The Rays, and others), the diverse topics with which Clair de Lune is aligned characterize this piece as a tabula rasa, a blank slate, ready to absorb meaning and signify a wide range of ideas and themes related to the moon and the night. We have seen how Debussy's simple yet alluring organization of musical components invites reinterpretation, while the undercurrent of suggestion that permeates Clair de Lune offers an even stronger pull on the listener's imagination. Even as intertextual relationships between Debussy's piece and its reworkings call attention to aspects of musical technique, it is ultimately an understated feeling of hesitation latent in Clair de Lune—of feelings left unexpressed and thoughts left unsaid—that continues to drive creative dialogue.

MOONLIGHT AND MARKETING IN COMMERCIALS

Underlying my discussion in this section is an observation by Timothy Taylor: "Music has power. Musicians know it, listeners know it. And so do advertisers." Like Taylor and Nicholas Cook, I explore how music works in the context of advertising, although my focus is quite different. While drawing attention to Clair de Lune's positive status as cliché, I show how the *same* piece of music is put in the service of a range of products, the sheer variety of which is mind-boggling.[24] McDonald's took advantage of the large audience watching the Oscars in 2015 by creating a clever commercial with an unlikely cast of characters: the ingredients of a Big Mac are intertwined with iconic Hollywood film dialogue set against Debussy's Clair de Lune.[25] The words and their syllables make an impact on viewers through careful synchronization with each musical gesture. (Listen to audio example 2.10 ▶.) At the *tempo rubato*, for instance, the second occurrence of the gesture that unfolds between measures 19 and 21 coincides with Robert De Niro's feisty line from *Taxi Driver*—"You talkin' to me?"—while the third occurrence (at m. 23) is placed alongside a word-for-word enunciation of the Big Mac's critical ingredients before the music fades away from the climax (mm. 25–26): "Two all-beef patties, special sauce, lettuce, cheese, pickles, onions . . ." The final marketing plug aligns transcendent-sounding music with the most magical part of the burger: soft, rising arpeggios underscore another set of famous last words: "on a sesame-seed bun." As if this wasn't slick enough, a shift of register to the McDonald's jingle in the final seconds of the ad effortlessly combines the jingle's reference to fast food advertising strategies of the twenty-first century with the sonic landscape of a piece from the beginning of the last century. Strangely, the two are not as distant as we might imagine. Conceived for the French marketplace, Clair de Lune was written with the cultural practices of Parisian society in mind; it was performed in small concert halls and in private salons as much as it would have been played at home, for fun. In much the same way, consumer culture and pleasure—albeit of the gastronomic variety—are also at the heart of how McDonald's continues to reinvent itself.

A consideration of pleasure brings into focus another concept with which Clair de Lune has come to be associated in the realm of advertising: luxury. The piece's French origins and its minimalist, subtle aesthetic have undoubtedly played a role in fostering this association. As a provider of luxury vehicles, Lexus has used the piece to promote technological innovation. For instance, the sport utility Lexus RX turned to Clair de Lune to underscore its contributions to the car industry in 2010.[26] The idea of classic luxury is emphasized through the use of Debussy's work in its original version for piano, as a father and his children navigate city traffic in the rain. Cocooned in their smooth-moving RX, the slow tempo and minimal melodic gestures of Debussy's introduction evoke a serene mood as driver and passengers look out at the less fortunate souls who are left in the rain to deal with the aggravations of city life. If the opening portion of Clair de Lune serves to establish an atmosphere of calm, the *tempo rubato*, with its sudden emphasis on E♭ minor triads and impassioned triplet chords, evokes a momentary feeling of suspense, which highlights the technological genius behind the inclusion of a GPS navigation system for avoiding traffic. The closing section, with its legato, rising and falling arpeggios (based on the *un poco mosso*), reveals the most impressive feature of the RX: it is an electric-powered car, whose smooth motion on the road is equated with the gossamer movement of the music's undulating sixteenth-note figuration. (Listen to audio example 2.11 ▶.) The quiet intimacy of Debussy's piece is used by Lexus to create a private world of luxury where life's most precious things (family and physical safety) are protected against the commotion of everyday life.

Yet another example of how Clair de Lune is tied to the realm of luxury by advertisers is an advertisement for the perfume Chanel No. 5. (Listen to audio example 2.12 ▶.) Nicole Kidman and Rodrigo Santoro appear in a dramatized commercial (a "mini-film" as Pam Cook calls it) directed by Baz Luhrmann in 2004, a few years after he had completed the movie *Moulin Rouge* (2001). The commercial captures the spirit of the movie.[27] Kidman, a renowned model whose reputation is known to everyone except Santoro, longs to escape from the glare of the paparazzi. As with *Moulin Rouge*, the narrative is initially presented from Santoro's point of view, as he reflects on his fateful romance from the shadowy rooftops of a pseudo–New York City skyscraper (à la Montmartre), while she must endure the perils of fame in the Chanel-logo-encrusted city below.[28]

Arranged by Craig Armstrong, the opening gestures of Clair de Lune are given a tragic hue through their recomposition in a minor key, where the eerie feel of the violins' high-pitched, sustained notes is reciprocated in the bare textures of the piano. Hollow chords accompany a wistful melody as a slowed-down sequence of fragmented scenes conveys the surreal, dreamlike existence into which the artist has fallen since meeting Kidman. "When did I awake into this dream?" Santoro asks himself at the opening. Armstrong's subtle rescoring of Debussy's work enhances the cinematic quality of the commercial by manipulating the music to work its magic in the background. Whereas Debussy's piece opens in D♭ major, Armstrong's shift to the minor mode signifies the tragic present, saving a shift to the major mode for when the artist recalls happy memories of the time he spent together with his love. He remembers Kidman's words, "It's beautiful up here; everything is so peaceful," an observation supported by the plush orchestration of the opening Clair de Lune statement. Trembling violins accompany whispered declarations of love, while the final section—with Kidman's vow, "No one can steal our dream, no one"—positions Clair de Lune within the world of romance, dream, and fantasy. This association is secured in the flowing arpeggios of the closing measures, as Kidman slowly ascends a red-carpeted staircase, stopping for a moment to look back at the artist as he sits wondering whether she still remembers him: "Has she forgotten? I know I will not . . . her kiss, her smile, her perfume." A sparkling diamond pendant "No. 5" glistens all the more on account of the shimmering orchestral colors of the violins, triangle, and harp.

Food, luxury vehicles, perfume: What is it that Clair de Lune brings to each of these contexts? Why might the directors behind these projects have wanted to use this gentle piano piece to reach their audiences? Responses on social networking sites such as YouTube show that while viewers were thinking about the marketed product, they were also, in some cases, *more* attuned to the atmosphere and mood conveyed by the use of Debussy's piece than to what was actually being sold. This is likely no coincidence, since Debussy was preoccupied with the challenge of how to connote atmosphere in music through most of his career. Even though one might claim that *all* music is capable of establishing a mood and provoking emotions or a range of feelings in listeners, Debussy's attention to affect is worth considering because it illuminates key aspects of his aesthetic ideals. Pausing now to reflect on *how* Debussy conjures atmosphere in his compositions will enable us to appreciate the musical techniques that formed the basis of his innovations, as well as the rules of composition he had to break in order to cultivate an intense yet subtle expressivity.

> Nothing is dearer than the grey song where the vague and
> the precise meet.
>
> > Paul Verlaine, "Art poétique," *Jadis et naguère* (1884)

Debussy's interest in honing an original compositional voice is already apparent in historical accounts of his time as a student at the Paris Conservatoire. One of his earliest biographers, Léon Vallas, documented the composer's "hatred of [music] theory and all its absurd rules," an opinion that is supported in school reports that alternate descriptions of Debussy as "gifted" and as "mischievous," qualities that are also emphasized in the reminiscences of his fellow classmates.[29] The type of originality that Debussy sought can be recognized in his methods for cultivating atmosphere. He wrote in 1913, "It is the musicians alone who have the privilege of being able to convey all the poetry of night and day, of earth and sky. Only they can re-create Nature's atmosphere and give rhythm to her heaving breast."[30] Debussy was mesmerized by the power of nature, whether witnessed in the physical world or in imagined forms of the sea, the countryside, the seasons, and meteorological elements (clouds, fog, rain). However, his soundscapes are not designed to depict nature with any degree of realism. To the contrary, his music aims to *stylize* nature, that is, to invoke the images and effects of nature as glimpsed during a passing moment in time.

Stylization is a useful term in this instance because it doesn't suggest a literal depiction; rather, it points to the gaps, the spaces that open up between an object (such as the moon), the sensory perception of that object (the moon as experienced in nature), and the transformation of the object as it passes through Debussy's imagination before being rendered as atmosphere in his work. As Debussy wrote in 1893, music "is not confined to an exact reproduction of nature, but only to the mysterious affinity between Nature and the Imagination."[31] The technique of stylization emphasizes a creative process where the artist uses his or her imagination to capture the mystery and beauty of nature. The pursuit of atmosphere is very much linked to the process of stylization, as explained by the first biographer of Debussy in English, Louise Liebich.

In her book from 1908, Liebich aligns Debussy's compositional methods with those of Impressionist painters, offering a discerning assessment of their attention to "the atmosphere which intervenes between . . . [observed] objects and themselves." Her observation directly invokes Claude Monet's remark of 1895: "To me the motif itself is an insignificant factor; what I want to reproduce is what lies between the motif and me."[32] Although the equation of Debussy's music with Impressionist art is persistent in how his music is marketed today, scholars have been wary of this parallel for some time, given its tendency to obfuscate and constrain our understanding of Debussy's innovations. Debussy himself was uneasy about this alignment: "In poetry and painting alike (and I managed to think of a couple of musicians as well) men had tried to shake away the dust of tradition . . . [but] it had only earned them the labels of 'symbolists' or 'impressionists'—useful terms of abuse."[33] Nonetheless, there is one respect in which Monet's art and Debussy's music profit from being compared, and this is with regard to their evocation of atmosphere.

In seeking to communicate the sensory richness of a single moment, Monet was intent on conveying what he called the *enveloppe*, that is, the "unifying atmosphere which surrounds objects," as described by the art historian John House.[34] A significant point of intersection between Monet and Debussy concerns their interest in stimulating the audience's sensory receptors to such an extent that the intangible, invisible realm of atmosphere may be felt as tangible and present, much as they perceived when viewing depictions of mist, fog, and the sky in the paintings of J. M. W. Turner and J. A. M. Whistler, admired by Monet and Debussy alike. Describing Turner as "the finest creator of mystery in the whole of art," Debussy looked to these painters' controversial methods for capturing the evanescence of nature in his own musical experiments.[35] Thus, Debussy's music transports its listeners to a state of contemplation, where perceived qualities of beauty and the ephemeral are not firmly embedded within a scene, but suffused through it, in the manner of atmosphere.

All in all, Debussy sought to create in sound the intense atmospheres he had experienced in the poetry of Mallarmé, the paintings of Turner and Whistler, and the drama of the Belgian Symbolist writer and playwright Maurice Maeterlinck. Mallarmé's famous phrase "To *name* an object is to suppress three-quarters of the enjoyment of the poem . . . to *suggest*, that is the dream," served as a mantra for these artists as they sought to render palpable something as evasive as atmosphere.[36] Even though atmosphere could not be seen, these innovators ensured it was always felt, and often in ways that proved disorienting for audiences. Debussy maintained that music could conjure atmosphere better than any other medium: "Music begins where speech fails," he wrote. "Music is intended to convey the inexpressible. I should like it to appear as if emerging from the shadowy regions to which it would from time to time retire."[37] Cinema was still in its infancy during Debussy's lifetime. He could not have imagined the extent to which Clair de Lune's shadowy luminescence would come to deepen his audience's immersion into the realm of fantasy.

LENDING ATMOSPHERE TO FILM

Debussy's page on the IMDb is teeming with examples of where his music has appeared in film and TV.[38] Clair de Lune is the most frequently cited composition whose use might be seen to fall into the cinematic categories of either diegetic (having a place within the storyline) or non-diegetic music (serving the role of background). Clair de Lune has been used to deepen the visual field of atmosphere, especially in contexts that invoke memory and recollection. Specifically, it has served to blur the distinction between diegetic and non-diegetic modes of narration by residing in a liminal space, one that the film music scholar Robynn Stilwell has called the "fantastical gap."[39] Although Clair de Lune is not unique in occupying this space—it is shared with such atmospheric stalwarts as Satie's *Gymnopédies* and Chopin's "Raindrop" Prelude, for instance—the manner in which the piece settles into and emerges from this space is what I explore in the following discussion.

The sense of unpredictability that comes from being "in between" endows the music of this space with an especially powerful expressive capability. Certainly, it is the paradoxical condition of being both background and foreground that is part of the allure for film directors. The naturally, self-effacing quality of Clair de Lune allows it to resist drawing attention to itself even when foregrounded. And yet the subtlety of Debussy's compositional approach ensures that it is always heard, even at moments where we might not be overtly cognizant of its presence (as music retreats into the shadows, or behind a veil, to recall Debussy's metaphors). The unmarked ways through which this piece works its way into our subconscious from the fantastical gap is ultimately what inspires visual media artists to explore how the dreamy and wistful quality of the piece has the potential to heighten the evocation of affect.

Some scholars have tended to frown upon the association of music with the creation of atmosphere, arguing that the perception of music as a background phenomenon is the reason why critical attention to the role of sound and music in cinema has been delayed.[40] As the following examples show, however, there is no need to be apologetic about how Clair de Lune functions to create atmosphere in film. While directors have clearly used the piece because of its atmospheric potential, these examples show that atmosphere is not a background phenomenon against which the narrative or personalities are developed. Atmosphere, as etched in both sonic and spatial dimensions by Clair de Lune, is a character in its own right, whose evocation of a range of feelings and emotions asks viewers to ponder the elusive relationship between music and affect. The examples that follow outline the circumscribed network of meanings within which Clair de Lune has been operating since its earliest affiliations with film. In this respect, Debussy's composition shares the same fate as that of another classical piece, Robert Schumann's "Traümerei." Jeremy Barham has shown how "Traümerei" also traveled "the path from intimate, well-formed, and semantically free-floating miniature at the center of an integrated collection, to segregated, mostly abridged or fragmented, object of mass exposure and semantically determined consumption."[41] In keeping with the multiple uses of "Traümerei," the discussion here highlights how the afterlife of a musical composition can fall far from the vision of its creator.

While Debussy's music was used to accompany silent films during the 1920s—the score for *The Cabinet of Dr. Caligari* features extracts from *Prélude à l'après-midi d'un faune*—Walt Disney was the first to realize the potential for visualization that lay in Clair de Lune, as seen in his initial plans for the animated film *Fantasia* (1940). (Listen to audio example 2.13 ⏵.)[42] Played by the Philadelphia Orchestra and conducted by Leopold Stokowski in his own arrangement, Debussy's music is accompanied by animated images of a full moon shining down on the sleepy swamps of a bayou.[43] The scene itself is magical and establishes many of the themes that continue to be associated with Clair de Lune: an elegant egret creates ripples in the water, flies through the dense foliage, and eventually pairs up with another egret, their silhouettes fading into the clouds as they fly toward the moon together. Disney was sensitive to the nuances of Debussy's piece: "It has the restful effect that we need. . . . You don't want too much effort in this—if you have too much going on then you don't hear it."[44] For fear of visual overload, Disney works with a fairly basic plot and a largely static set of visuals to engage his viewers. In this regard, Stokowski's plush orchestration has an important role to play, given how the sentimental strings invite us to anthropomorphize the egret such that the opening mood of loneliness and melancholy easily gives way to one of love and optimism (figure 2.1).

Fantasia was initially released without the Clair de Lune animation sequence, which was cut on account of the film's length. Interestingly, the original animation for the film's Clair de Lune sequence was issued in *Make Mine Music* (1946), a collection of shorts brought out by Disney after the Second World War, where instead of being accompanied by Debussy's work, the sequence was renamed "Blue Bayou" and supported by music composed by Bobby Worth and Ray Gilbert and performed by the Ken Darby Chorus. By this time, Debussy's Clair de Lune was well known to concertgoing American audiences. While Disney was

FIGURE 2.1   From Walt Disney's *Fantasia* (uncut version).

among the first to align Debussy's sound with image, his decision to intertwine this piece with a Floridian landscape created a distinctly American setting for Clair de Lune that overlooked its French origins. Disney's efforts to market classical music for middle-class American audiences were paralleled by an interest in adapting Debussy's music for the silver screen, where its manipulation in situations concerning love, heartbreak, and nostalgia deepened its connection to American emotionalism.[45]

Although Clair de Lune had featured in a film as early as 1934—the dancer Sally Rand performed her famous fan dance to this music in Wesley Ruggles's *Bolero*—it is only after the Second World War that we see it being taken up again as a musical topic in three films that appeared in quick succession: *Frenchman's Creek* (1944) (based on the novel by Daphne du Maurier), *Music for Millions* (1945), and *Without Love* (1945). Victor Young's orchestration of Clair de Lune in *Frenchman's Creek* offers it up as a love theme that shadows how Dona St. Columb (Joan Fontaine), an aristocratic Englishwoman, falls in love with a French pirate, Jean Benoit Aubrey (Arturo de Córdova). While Clair de Lune signifies romantic intimacy, Annegret Fauser has recently shown how this music also identifies a broad notion of Frenchness, which extends to the pirate's ship and his crew. Fauser notes how the otherwise introspective music of Clair de Lune is masculinized by being transformed "into something approaching a military fanfare," as befitting the political situation of the moment.[46]

Set during the Second World War, *Music for Millions* explores the association between romantic longing and Clair de Lune through diegetic performance. (Listen to audio example 2.14 ▶.) While José Iturbi plays the opening of Clair de Lune during an orchestra rehearsal, Larry Adler's version for harmonica is particularly memorable: Barbara Ainsworth (June Allyson) requests the performance in memory of her missing husband, who is away at war. Before Adler begins his performance, he asks her: "You won't bawl the way you did last time?" Barbara gives due assurance. But soon after he begins his performance, accompanied by violins and piano, the camera moves slowly across the crowd before pausing on Barbara, who finds herself gradually welling up as the music reaches the middle section. Clair de Lune's association with heartbreak is especially poignant in this scene, given how it unlocks a suppressed fear that she will never see her husband again.[47]

A similar psychological function is assigned to the piece in *Without Love*, where Clair de Lune is played on the piano by Pat Jamieson (Spencer Tracy), whose tendency to sleepwalk has led him to the grand piano in the luxurious home of Jamie Rowan (Katharine Hepburn). After pulling back the drapes to let the moonlight filter in through gauze curtains, Pat, still standing, plays the opening notes. He quickly settles in to play an abridged version of the piece, which awakens Jamie and stirs her emotions; as she stands outside the room, large tears roll down her cheeks (figures 2.2a and 2.2b). The ensuing conversation about lost love once again establishes a correlation between Debussy's piece and heartbreak, which is explored with an unusual degree of intimacy here. As noted by Lawrence Weingarten, "It was the first time . . . someone played 'Clair de Lune' properly, not the vamped up [orchestral] version."[48] In a later film, *Giant* (1956), Clair de Lune is linked with

FIGURE 2.2A *Without Love*: Spencer Tracy plays Clair de Lune.

FIGURE 2.2B *Without Love*: Katharine Hepburn listens.

feelings of nostalgia. Uncle Bawley (Chill Wills) plays an unusually scored version for organ while Leslie Benedict (Elizabeth Taylor) reflects on her unsatisfying life at a Texas ranch through snippets of conversation with Bawley while he plays.

Early on, Hollywood set a precedent for associating Clair de Lune with romantic longing and nostalgia. In the late sixties, these themes were taken up again, although in a comedic setting. In the opening few minutes of *Casino Royale* (1967), a spoof in the James Bond tradition, the British spy is introduced as an eccentric figure who keeps lions and "plays Debussy every afternoon from sunset until it's too dark to read the news." James Bond (David Niven) proves this point when he interrupts a meeting with leading international spies—"If I may interrupt this furl of cliché, it is now that time of day I have set apart for Debussy"—after which the camera cuts to a scene where Bond is seated at the piano in the throes of the *un poco mosso* played at a remarkably brisk tempo so that the music sounds unusually virtuosic. As strains of Clair de Lune waft through the grounds, doubts are raised over his capabilities as a spy:

"Can this be the man who won a Victoria Cross at Mafeking?"
"The hero of the Ashanti Uprising?"
"What genius is wasted in the face of a crumbling empire!"

Bond's love for Mata Hari is revealed to be the source of his pain and the reason for his exclusion from the spy world. Only the music of Debussy can assuage his pain, a point reiterated later in a hilarious moment, when his archrival Dr. Noah / Jimmy Bond (Woody Allen) plays the same passage from Clair de Lune while trying to convince a captive female agent of his manliness and thus resemblance to James Bond.

The unlikely appearance of Clair de Lune within the genre of satire anticipates several other unusual contexts in which the piece later finds itself. Most closely related is Wes Anderson's comedy *Darjeeling Limited* (2007), where Clair de Lune is heard soon after the three brothers are thrown off a train traveling through India in the middle of the night. (Listen to audio example 2.15 ▶.) "Let's get high" is Francis's cue for Peter and Jack (played by Owen Wilson, Adrien Brody, and Jason Schwartzman, respectively) to pass around medicinal substances that they pipette into their mouths before contemplating forlorn relationships with their mother and each other.[49] As they sit in the dark, Clair de Lune provides a sonic manifestation of moonlight that touches each of the brothers: "Maybe this is how it's supposed to happen. Could all be a part of it. Maybe this is where the spiritual journey ends," says the youngest brother, Jack. Sounding from out of the fantastical gap, this music urges the brothers to express their innermost thoughts and anxieties while contemplating their place in the world.

Another unexpected yet effective use of Clair de Lune is found in the vampire horror series *Twilight* (2008). Inspired by Stephenie Meyer's novels, the first movie of the Twilight Saga draws on Clair de Lune to create a moment of intimacy between an awkward teenager, Bella (Kristen Stewart), and Edward, the vampire to whom she is drawn (Robert Pattinson). Meyer emphasizes the atmospheric qualities of Debussy's music in her novel, where Clair de Lune encourages dreamy contemplation of the rain.

> I was preparing to give him the silent treatment—my face in full pout mode—but then I recognized the music playing, and my curiosity got the better of my intentions.
>
> "Clair de Lune?" I asked, surprised. "You know Debussy?" He sounded surprised, too.
>
> "Not well," I admitted. "My mother plays a lot of classical music around the house—I only know my favorites."
>
> "It's one of my favorites, too." He stared out through the rain, lost in thought.
>
> I listened to the music, relaxing against the light gray leather seat. It was impossible not to respond to the familiar, soothing melody. The rain blurred everything outside the window into gray and green smudges. I began to realize we were driving very fast; the car moved so steadily, so evenly, though, I didn't feel the speed. Only the town flashing by gave it away.[50]

Debussy's music functions differently in the movie *Twilight*, where it is heard in the privacy of Edward's bedroom after he has introduced Bella to his family. Bella recognizes the music and in so doing creates the first step toward striking an even deeper personal connection with the vampire. Edward and Bella attempt to dance to Clair de Lune before he decides to take her out for a ride—on his back, soaring into the sky and through the trees. In this scene, Debussy's music shifts from a diegetic to a fantastical space, as Bella transitions into a realm where teenage girls fly and fall in love with vampires.

Associations with dreaming and escape are especially poignant in *Seven Years in Tibet* (1997), based on Heinrich Harrer's novel about China's political relationship with

Tibet. The film opens with a ceremony where the young Dalai Lama receives a charming little music box, which, when opened, plays a quasi-pentatonic rendition of Clair de Lune.[51] The Dalai Lama is entranced by the music and the beautifully adorned box, whose cover displays the Tibetan flag. He returns to the music as a source of refuge when he is a little older and struggling to protect his country from Chinese occupation: "I'm hiding from the world for a day," is what the young Dalai Lama says to Harrer (Brad Pitt) as Debussy's music takes him away from the political turmoil in which he is entrenched. As Harrer is leaving for Austria, the Dalai Lama places the cloth-wrapped music box into his hands. Harrer passes it on to his son from whom he has been estranged for some time. Debussy's Clair de Lune thus serves as a source of delight and wonder for another young boy, bringing him to a closer understanding of himself, as reflected in the final scene, where father and son hike together in the Himalayas.

Interpretations of Clair de Lune as offering a means of escape find a powerful connection to trauma in two other films: *Atonement* (2007) and *The Right Stuff* (1983). In *Atonement*, Briony Tallis (Romola Garai), a wealthy aristocrat turned nurse in the Second World War, finds herself tending to the fatal wounds of a dying soldier, Luc Cornet (Jérémie Renier). At a climactic moment, the film takes up a thread from the novel by Ian McEwan on which it is based: Luc remembers Briony's older sister, Cecilia (Keira Knightly), and her love for the housekeeper's son, Robbie (James McAvoy), a memory that sparks regret in Briony, since the atonement she seeks in her life results from her jealous efforts to separate Cecilia and Robbie. In between his hallucinations, Luc recalls his life at Millau, and he remembers the time Briony visited the family bakery. He speaks of his sister, Anne: "She's the prettiest girl in Millau. She passed her grade exam with a tiny piece by Debussy, so full of light and fun."[52] Seconds later, as soon as Luc passes away, Clair de Lune is heard in its version for piano as Briony walks down the ward, blood from tending to Luc's bandages smeared on her face, shock running through her body. The serene music merges Luc's final recollections of his sister's Debussy with a morale-boosting film being shown to hospitalized soldiers in a separate ward. Without blinking, Briony blankly observes footage of smiling soldiers celebrating victory at Dunkirk with the same wide-eyed stare that witnessed Luc's last sighs. The fantastical beauty of Debussy's music is now heard as strangely other-worldly, not in the sense of myth and dream (as in *Twilight*) but as music whose poignant entry at the moment of Luc's death haunts every smile and allows the commentator's rhetorical propaganda, heard in the background, to ring cold and hollow: "The army is undefeated. Courage has brought them through unconquered, their spirit unbowed. This is the epic of Dunkirk, a name that will live forever in the annals of warfare."

The link between trauma and Debussy's music is intensified in *The Right Stuff*, where an orchestral version of Clair de Lune provides the musical accompaniment for Sally Rand's famous feather dance, which used to draw crowds to her performances at the Chicago World's Fair of 1933–34.[53] Performed here by Peggy Davis, the dance is featured at an event inaugurating the Manned Spacecraft Center in Houston honoring the Mercury Seven group of astronauts. (Listen to audio example 2.16 ▶.)[54] Although Rand dances to "Sugar Blues" in Tom Wolfe's novel, *The Right Stuff*, the director Philip Kaufman chooses the ethereal quality of Debussy's music to underscore the lightness of Rand's giant ostrich feathers as they glide through the air and envelop her (apparently) naked body. In combination with the free-flowing movements of Rand's dance, the music encourages daydreaming, and thus it facilitates a subtle transition from the diegetic into a fantastical space: the astronauts initially lose themselves in the whiteness of the feathers, as they merge with the white glare of the enormous spherical floor light whose symbolic connection to the moon also correlates with the determination of Chuck Yeager (played by Sam Shepard) to "punch a hole in the sky." As sound, motion, and light converge, Yeager is catapulted from a state of dreamy reverie into one of traumatic recall, as he remembers an earlier failed attempt to break the sound barrier, during which he nearly lost his life. In parallel, the astronauts, while distracted by Clair de Lune and its visual counterpart in shadow theater dance, glance knowingly at one another, taking time to reflect on the significance of their accomplishments as members of the Mercury Seven.

Bonds of unity and brotherhood are also felt within the sound world of Clair de Lune shown in a film written in the heist genre, Steven Soderbergh's *Ocean's Eleven* (2001). (Listen to audio example 2.17 ▶.) Following a fairly intense few hours of master criminals taking on the biggest casinos of Las Vegas, Clair de Lune enters gently in the final few scenes (having already been heard at two earlier moments of the film).[55] In an orchestral arrangement by Lucien

Cailliet, the slow tempo and metric fluidity of Debussy's music shift the film toward a different temporal plane, where seemingly static expressions conceal a multitude of competing thoughts.[56] For example, Terry Benedict's resolute stare as he watches Tess Ocean leave (played, respectively, by Andy Garcia and Julia Roberts) is accompanied by music from the *tempo rubato*. The counterpart to Terry's iron-melting glare is the composed look of contentment on the faces of the eleven after they arrive at the Bellagio. As their eyes feast on the splendid display of the fountains glimpsed against the backdrop of the illuminated mini Eiffel Tower, we hear a richly orchestrated return of the opening melody. Also relevant is Tess's outward gaze after leaving Terry. Looking past the crowds, she struts determinedly through the casino, her rapid gait matched to the undulating motion of the *un poco mosso* as she scurries to bid farewell to the man she still loves, her ex-husband, Danny Ocean (George Clooney). In this instance, Clair de Lune's fading arpeggiation is used once again to denote love and heartbreak.

A compelling example of how a seemingly vacant expression can say more than words is seen in the final few minutes of the film, where the closing section of Debussy's piece underscores each member's speechless appreciation of the Bellagio's famous fountains, which also translates into admiration for their collective genius. Soderbergh seems to have had Verlaine's poem close at hand, as seen in his efforts to align Debussy's closing music with the swaying dance of the fountains before synchronizing the final luminescent chord—especially sumptuous in its scoring for strings, harp, and woodwinds—with an explosive array of sound and color as the fountains ascend to the grand heights of the Bellagio's faux marble façade. We recall Verlaine's final stanza: "With the calm moonlight sad and beautiful, which makes the birds dream in the trees, and the fountains sob with ecstasy, the tall slender fountains among the marbles" (see companion website for the full text of Verlaine's "Clair de Lune" ▶). This moment is quiet and sad with Verlaine but jubilant and transcendent with Soderbergh, not to mention briefly ironic, as signaled by the sight of the gaudy Bellagio fountains traversing the kitschy Las Vegas landscape (figure 2.3).

Together, these examples show some of the various ways in which Clair de Lune has been used in film to highlight themes ranging from romantic longing, heartbreak, nostalgia, and intimacy to trauma, escapism, and transcendence. And one could easily find many more: *Frankie and Johnny* (1991) features a non-diegetic Clair de Lune to reveal bonds of intimacy between estranged lovers; *Dog Soldiers* (2002) relies on a diegetic appearance that creates a cocoon of safety to contrast with the daily grind

FIGURE 2.3 *Ocean's Eleven*: Verlaine's fountains at the Bellagio.

of hunting werewolves; in *Man on Fire* (2004), Debussy's music intrudes in a fantastical way upon a suicide scene to function as a sonic sign sent from the universe; Federico Fellini's late film *And the Ship Sails On* (1983) makes diegetic use of Clair de Lune in an arrangement for wordless voice and piano, whose setting highlights the decline of European aristocracy.

The ubiquitous presence of Clair de Lune in film as well as in commercials demonstrates how a piece of music that tells us we need food, cars, and perfume can also invite us to empathize with a range of feelings, emotions, and psychological states—a multiplicity (or flexibility) of meaning that draws our attention to the subtle nuances of Debussy's writing. Every new reinterpretation reminds us of how Debussy's music has the remarkable ability to move listeners and viewers across time and space, even those who might not otherwise think of themselves as connoisseurs of classical music.

FEELING TOGETHER IN VIDEO GAMES

Considering the use of Clair de Lune in video games steers the discussion in a different direction, for it prompts investigation of how this type of music invites participants to engage with and control its presence. In this section, I'll aim to extend a conversation that is already ongoing in online communities, as evidenced in discussions about the piece on blogs and social networking sites. These virtual exchanges offer notable insights into those aspects of Debussy's composition that players find remarkably moving. Especially striking in these dialogues is how Clair de Lune serves to create unifying bonds between strangers, for whom the act of play leads to a larger awareness of how dispersed communities of players can be touched by the same music.

Recent scholarship in digital media has begun to address the issue of how certain pieces have the potential to enrich the physical, psychological, and emotional experience of playing video games. Although the impact of Clair de Lune has not yet been examined along these lines by scholars, we will see that it is one such piece. As seen in YouTube comments, fans of this music often recognize it as the "song" from Shinji Mikami's *The Evil Within* (2014), where it emanates from safe havens, specifically the gleaming mirrors that invite the player (under the avatar of Sebastian Castellanos) toward them. In an otherwise tension-ridden game filled with blood and gore where the player must defeat zombie-like creatures, Debussy's piece offers respite and a means of momentary escape (a function we saw in *Dog Soldiers* and *Seven Years in Tibet*), but only if the player allows her avatar to take the opportunity to reflect. If she does, what can be heard is a version of Clair de Lune arranged for violin and piano where the music is manipulated to sound as though it is coming from an old, scratched LP. In this scoring, Debussy's music has a certain plaintive quality that some might hear as restorative and meditative, although, as Phil Savage explains in an article for *PC Gamer*, the effect is quite temporary: " 'This is nice,' I think, as a man limps and stumbles through a corridor. That's the power of Debussy for you. Clair de Lune can make anything seem serene. Don't worry, it doesn't last."[57] The dazzling mirror makes visible the fantastical space from which the soothing sounds of Clair de Lune beckon the player; as Castellanos gazes at his reflection, he enters the deep recesses of his troubled mind, which brings to the fore questions of whether his battle takes place in the real world or in the fantastical realm of his nightmares. Even within the genre of survival horror, it is striking that, over any other piece of music, it is Clair de Lune that compels the listener to look inward in pondering questions concerning their identity and existence.

The relationship between music and atmosphere that we explored in relation to film is also pertinent to the format of video games, as examined by Gregor Herzfeld, who explains how "the controlled application of music in genres of mixed media [allows] the producer [to make] use of its power to evoke, strengthen or express affective content in a very direct way." Herzfeld views composers of video game music as offering "a framework of aural atmosphere to the product and to help complete the user's mood management."[58] This effort is evident in *Rain*, a game conceived by Makoto Shinkai in 2013, in which the player's avatar is a recently deceased young boy who runs around a derelict city trying to find the little girl whose ghostly silhouette he had seen earlier.[59] The rain plays an important role in this game. As we saw in Meyer's novel *Twilight*, rain serves to prolong a mood of introspection and dreaming, one that is enhanced by visual emphasis on hues of black and gray in Shinkai's visual design. The faint outline of the boy plays off these cool colors, and against the sound of thick, heavy raindrops. The supernatural aura of the game is enhanced by the fact that the rain renders the world of spirits visible. When the rain is absent—when the boy finds momentary shelter, for instance—he is rendered invisible. This is only a problem when he tries to find company—loneliness is the prevailing emotional state with which Clair de Lune is associated in *Rain*—because he is constantly being chased by spectral monsters of the night.

The evocation of atmosphere is central to Shinkai's conception of *Rain*, a preoccupation that probably has much to do with his background in Japanese anime and film. From the point of view of game play, it is interesting that some players have found the atmospheric quality of *Rain* to be immensely moving, while others have cited this same dimension as a flaw.[60] The composer, Yugo Kanno, explains: "This is one of the more peaceful projects I've worked on. We tried to reflect that in the music, giving it an artistic serenity, and avoiding any noticeable climaxes or builds, but instead having it kind of pervade the experience throughout."[61] Clair de Lune seems to have been a perfect choice in this regard. Kanno was asked to augment the atmospheric qualities of Debussy's piece by adding a vocal part for a young girl (sung by Connie Talbot, a finalist in *Britain's Got Talent*, 2007), presumably correlating with the voice of the girl befriended by the boy in *Rain*. The conflation of Debussy's composition with Kanno's song "A Tale" injects an additional narrative layer, which solidifies the dreamy quality of Debussy's piece, with its longstanding link to love and yearning. A feeling of vulnerability, deepened through the non-diegetic use of Clair de Lune, also highlights the quality of precarity central to Shinkai's work.[62]

Players of *Rain* are asked to attend to the nuances of the atmosphere, and thus to engage in a variety of play that is relatively aimless, a point of frustration for those who seek a more involved level of interaction. A similar criticism greeted *Adrift* (2016), where the commercial trailer uses Clair de Lune to heighten the effects of virtual reality as a lone female astronaut (Commander Alex Oshima) drifts through space amidst the wreckage of a space station. (Listen to audio example 2.18 .)[63] Critical reviews of the game describe its strong points in terms that relate to Debussy's prefacing music: the game offers "strong atmosphere," "a sense of weightlessness," "an excuse to gently float around in a beautifully ruined space station."[64] Interestingly, Clair de Lune's overriding associations with serenity and dreaming direct the player's attention to aspects of visual space and texture; as noted by Stephany Nunneley, "Adrıft is rather gorgeous on its own. But when you combine such loveliness with Claude Debussy's tranquil Clair de Lune, you'd assume the game would be a pleasant, relaxing experience. But you'd be wrong." While Debussy's music accompanies beautiful views of Earth and a nauseatingly real experience of being able to see objects from unusual viewpoints—given the ability to rotate 360 degrees in a gravityless environment—it detracts from this clichéd function by exacerbating the dissonance between soothing sound and otherworldly image.

However far video and cinematic uses of Clair de Lune might appear to take the work from Debussy's original conception, their cultivation of an immersive experience where sound comes to inflect the act of viewing was one to which Debussy was also attuned. "What a real joy it was to be able to listen to music without anxiety," he wrote, "to feel an atmosphere of joy surrounding you and becoming ever stronger, till in the end you weren't sure whether you really existed, and whether you hadn't turned into that menacing timpani roll or that harmonic on the cello."[65] When placed alongside the visual examples discussed here, Debussy's admiration of a mode of listening in which we lose our sense of self might help us understand why producers and designers return time and again to his techniques for composing atmosphere through sound. Despite Debussy's lack of interest in Clair de Lune, the diverse ways it has been claimed across popular culture underscore the point that repetition permits clichés to accrue expressive force. The emphasis upon originality as a measure of genius in traditional Western aesthetics has allowed cliché to be dismissed as little more than an irritation, a sign that betrays an anxiety of influence, as argued by the literary theorist Ryan Stark.[66] Rather than view cliché in negative terms as "a blank," however, this condition is a source of strength for Clair de Lune, where blankness serves as a tabula rasa. Viewed from this perspective, Debussy's Clair de Lune seems to say to each listener, "Make me yours"—an invitation that has undoubtedly contributed to its fame and ubiquity.[67]

At the same time that Clair de Lune establishes this level of intimacy, the commercial success of the musical and visual examples discussed in this chapter suggests another function of cliché discussed by Stark: its ability to create "powerful connective pathos," a deep psychological and emotional connection between creative figures and their audiences as they coalesce around a single piece of music.[68] In this chapter, we have seen how acceptance of

Clair de Lune's status as cliché allows different media and techniques to be brought into proximity with one another, while encouraging artists and their audiences to ponder humankind's fascination with the moon and its many meanings.

CHAPTER 3

THE *SUITE BERGAMASQUE* TAKES SHAPE

T HIS BRIEF CHAPTER HAS two goals: to position Clair de Lune within the larger historical and stylistic context of the *Suite Bergamasque* and, in so doing, to reflect on the various meanings of the title. Even though many listeners recognize Debussy's short composition for piano, few know it as the third movement of a larger multimovement work, and even fewer are aware of the significance of the title, *Bergamasque*, for Clair de Lune. The present discussion serves as a pivot point for the book: in contrast to the broad overview of the previous chapter, the narrow focus here paves the way for a deeper analytical and cultural appreciation of Debussy's famous work.

Since the compositional history of the *Suite Bergamasque* is somewhat convoluted, this chapter will begin by offering a succinct summary of the sequence of events that took place between the time it was conceived and the moment of its publication some fifteen years later. That the suite was published at all, and with this specific configuration of movements, is somewhat fortuitous. The haphazard circumstances surrounding its completion provide useful insights into Debussy's approach to composition, including his flexible attitude with respect to providing titles for pieces, the way he settled on their final position within multimovement works, and his borrowing of musical material from his own compositions, as well as those of others. The musicologists Roy Howat and Robert Orledge have undertaken extensive research on the history of the *Suite Bergamasque*.[1] I will build on their findings before giving an overview of each movement, my goal being to highlight how Clair de Lune stands apart from the other movements of the set as the lyrical highpoint of the entire suite.

HUMBLE BEGINNINGS

When the suite was first envisioned around 1890, Debussy was still a young composer with little to his public name beyond some songs, the compositions that had secured his success in the Prix de Rome competition, and some attempts at dramatic music. He was likely paid in advance for the suite by the publisher Antoine Choudens in February 1891. With no piano music yet published, Debussy was keen to get to work and started to make plans for a four-movement composition. It is possible that the suite at this time was comprised of a Prélude, Menuet, Promenade Sentimentale, and Pavane (version 1, figure 3.1).

SUITE BERGAMASQUE VERSION 1 (1890)

MOVEMENT 1	MOVEMENT 2	MOVEMENT 3	MOVEMENT 4
Prélude	Menuet	Promenade Sentimentale	Pavane

SUITE BERGAMASQUE VERSION 2 (1903) 3-movement Suite as advertised by Fromont:

MOVEMENT 1	MOVEMENT 2	MOVEMENT 3
Masques	2e Sarabande (D'un cahier d'esquisses)	L'île joyeuse

SUITE BERGAMASQUE FINAL VERSION (1905) as published by Fromont:

MOVEMENT 1	MOVEMENT 2	MOVEMENT 3	MOVEMENT 4
Prélude	Menuet	Clair de Lune	Passepied

FIGURE 3.1   The evolution of the *Suite Bergamasque*.

Four years later, the suite remained unpublished. Georges Hartmann bought the suite from Choudens in 1895 with the aim of publishing it, but Debussy's promises of newer music distracted Hartmann from this task. Having recently completed the *Prélude à l'après-midi d'un faune*, Debussy was also preoccupied with the initial plans for his opera, *Pelléas et Mélisande*, and the *Trois Nocturnes*. When Hartmann died unexpectedly in 1900, his heir, Général Bourgeat, not only demanded that Debussy return the advances Hartmann had paid him but also decided to sell some of Debussy's compositions, including the rights to those that were still in progress (like the *Suite Bergamasque*), to the publisher Fromont in 1902.

Fromont did not immediately publish the suite. The publishing house put out advertisements between 1903 and 1904, announcing a three-movement *Suite Bergamasque* that was entirely different from the first version (figure 3.2). As shown in figure 3.1, version 2 included as its first movement Masques, followed by a sarabande—Howat has argued that this eventually became D'un cahier d'esquisses—closing with L'île joyeuse (as it was spelled at the time). Debussy eventually sold Masques and L'Isle joyeuse (respelled during revisions in the summer of 1904 following his sojourn with Emma Bardac to the Isle of Jersey) to Durand. Durand then published Masques and L'Isle joyeuse as individual pieces. D'un cahier d'esquisses was eventually published by Schott in Brussels, having first appeared in the journal *Paris illustré* in February 1904.

With these pieces sold off, Debussy could well have abandoned the idea of the suite, but his financial circumstances prevented him from doing so. In March and April 1905, he edited and polished the earlier pieces of 1890 (the Prélude, Menuet, and Pavane) and likely put finishing touches on Clair de Lune, which was either a retitling of or a replacement for the original third movement, the Promenade Sentimentale. The final *Suite Bergamasque* as we know it today is this third version. By insisting that the date 1890 be printed directly under the title, Debussy ensured that it would be seen as a product of his youth, although he needn't have worried, given the stylistic distance between the suite and such recently composed works as *Estampes* (1903) and *L'isle joyeuse* (1904).

Since sketches of Clair de Lune are not available for consultation, it is hard to know whether the piece began life in 1890 as Promenade Sentimentale or if it was newly composed sometime in the early 1900s. Motivic overlaps with

Claude DEBUSSY

Pièces pour le PIANO

A la Fontaine, de SCHUMANN, extraite des 12 pièces à 4 mains (op. 85), transcription . . . . 2 »
Ballade. 2.50
Danse. . . . . 2 »
Images. . . . . 5 »
Mazurka. . . . . 2 »
Pour le Piano : Prélude, Sarabande, Toccata. . . . . 6 »
Rêverie. 1.75
Suite Bergamasque : Masques, 2ᵉ Sarabande, l'ile joyeuse . . 5 »
Valse Romantique. 2.50

PIANO ET ORCHESTRE - PIANO 4 MAINS
DEUX PIANOS

Fantaisie pour Piano et Orchestre, en deux parties . . . . . . » »
Marche Écossaise sur un thème populaire, à 4 mains . . . . 3 »
Trois Nocturnes : NUAGES, FÊTES, SIRÈNES, réduction à deux pianos . . . . 15 »
Prélude à l'après-midi d'un Faune, réduction à deux pianos . . . . 6 »

TOUS CES PRIX SONT NETS

PARIS — E. FROMONT, Éditeur, Rue d'Anjou, 40 (Boulevard Malesherbes)
Tous droits d'exécution, de traduction, de reproduction et d'arrangements réservés pour tous pays, y compris la Suède, la Norvège et le Danemark.   London, SCHOTT et Cⁱᵉ, 157, Regent Street.

FIGURE 3.2   Fromont advertises version 2 of the *Suite Bergamasque*. Claude Debussy, *Marche écossaise*, The Morgan Library & Museum. PMC 998.

contemporaneous pieces—his own *Petite Suite* and Gabriel Fauré's song "Clair de Lune"—suggest the former. As shown in example 3.1, in the Prélude, Debussy transforms a motif from measure 18 of Fauré's "Clair de Lune" into a whole-tone figure in measures 33–34, the outline of which is also reminiscent

EXAMPLE 3.1   A motif from Fauré's "Clair de Lune" is transformed in the Prélude, the Menuet, and En bateau.

of the whole-tone noodling from the first movement of his own *Petite Suite* (En bateau, Seconda, mm. 69–70).

This same whole-tone pattern is found at several moments of the next movement of the *Suite Bergamasque*, the Menuet, (see m. 2), whose title creates a link with Fauré's song, which is subtitled "Menuet." Fauré's presence can also be felt in the sudden name change of the Pavane to Passepied. It happened late and was possibly an effort to avert fingers pointing to Fauré's *Pavane* (1886–87) as a source of influence (which it clearly was, as seen in the choice of key and the thematic similarity between the left-hand figuration that opens both pieces).

The cyclic treatment of material within the *Suite Bergamasque* supports the theory that Clair de Lune was sketched around the same time as the other pieces of the suite. For example, the eighth-plus-two-sixteenths rhythm of the thirds motif from measure 11 of the Prélude is rendered through rhythmic diminution as a sixteenth and two thirty-seconds in measure 5 of the Menuet. Debussy then treats the Prélude's thirds motif through rhythmic augmentation at the opening of Clair de Lune (see example 3.2).

If indeed Clair de Lune is contemporaneous with the other pieces of the suite, it seems that Debussy singled the movement out for special treatment. It is conceived in the spirit of poetry, whereas the titles of the other movements assign them to a tradition of keyboard practice favored at the court of King Louis XIV by the harpsichordist and composer François Couperin and later continued by Jean-Philippe Rameau, both composers whom Debussy came to adore. When Debussy invokes the forms of the eighteenth-century French keyboard suite in the Prélude, Menuet, and Passepied, he

EXAMPLE 3.2 Motivic transformation from the Prélude through the Menuet to Clair de Lune.

pays homage to the past while using characteristic musical gestures to edge his way into new stylistic terrain.

The Prélude, for instance, opens with an arabesque flourish, which speaks to the improvisatory nature of ornamentation in the music of Couperin and Rameau. This melody embodies a contour beloved by Debussy that was to become a sort of musical signature, given its regular occurrence throughout his oeuvre. Here, its tumbling profile inspires new decorative figuration heard at measure 26, where rhythmic and virtuosic complexity—the pianist has to enact a seamless transition as she crosses hands to complete the gesture—looks ahead to the advanced pianistic techniques developed in later piano pieces. Even as we are drawn to the radically new textures inspired by the arabesque, other parts of the Prélude point to Debussy's training in traditional compositional techniques of counterpoint and part writing.

The Menuet also invokes the art of French Baroque harpsichordists through its intricate ornamentation and reams of undulating thirds. Despite the coy opening, this movement offers more than a mere tribute to the past. Debussy asserts his compositional hand in a number of ways. Quite unexpectedly, he places metric emphasis on the second beat, somewhat in the manner of a sarabande, but also setting the stage for numerous opportunities to create metric ambiguity (mm. 5–8, for instance, sound like three measures in 4/4 meter). In this movement, Debussy contrasts contrapuntal textures with those that privilege block chords, an innovation praised by several of his early critics in reaction to his maturing style. Furthermore, as the piece gains momentum, the intensification of the dynamics and broadening tessitura mark an important transformation, as the disciplined harpsichord of the opening evolves into a powerful piano whose wide range is emphasized in the closing four-octave rising glissando. Attacked with an accented sforzando but reclining immediately into a barely audible pianississimo, this counterintuitive gesture is one of Debussy's many attempts to create humor in music. The Passepied prolongs the playful quality of the Menuet through its perpetual ostinato eighth-note pattern. Despite its roots in Fauré's *Pavane*, the serene mood of Fauré's piece remains distant from Debussy's bustling final movement.

Given the intricate ornamentation of the Prélude, the motivic richness of the Menuet, and the rhythmic energy of the Passepied, how does Clair de Lune fit into the suite as a whole? While subtle musical interconnections establish a sense of continuity through the suite, Debussy's decision to follow the closing Aeolian scale of the Menuet with the distant key of D♭ major and a relaxed compound meter (9/8) casts Clair de Lune as an oasis of calm in a composition that is otherwise bursting with a diversity of textures and figurations. Like many expressive slow movements, Clair de Lune also marks a moment of repose in the suite, as the simple beauty of Debussy's arpeggios and rippling thirds attune our ears to the warm timbres and uniquely sonorous, sustained sound synonymous with his piano compositions today.

DEBUSSY'S CHOICE OF TITLE

The name *Bergamasque* would bring Debussy and Fauré together later in their careers as well, as seen in their efforts to render the topic of the *bergamasque* through dramatic presentation. Around 1909–10, Debussy, together with the musicologist Louis Laloy, engaged in dialogue with Sergei Diaghilev of the Ballets Russes about creating a ballet based on the commedia dell'arte, to be called *Masques et Bergamasques*. In the end, Debussy usurped Laloy by writing the scenario himself, much to Laloy's chagrin. But little of the music was completed.[2] In contrast, Fauré composed music for a divertissement also called *Masques et Bergamasques*, which was premiered in Monte Carlo in 1919. Paul Verlaine's "Clair de Lune" seems also to have inspired Fauré, as seen in his quotation of lines from the poem when describing the music of his own *Masques et Bergamasques* to his wife: it gives "the same sort of impression as a Watteau which Verlaine has defined so well."[3]

By the time Debussy decided to name his suite, the term *bergamasque* was part of a rich network of meanings. As seen with Shakespeare, it was associated with a dance, the Bergomask, which is performed at the end of *A Midsummer Night's Dream*. This rustic dance had its origins in a sixteenth-century folk dance (*bergamasco*) originating in the northern Italian town of Bergamo, for which the accompanying instruments would have played a fixed harmonic progression. This practice led to composers writing *bergamasca* melodies, those that could be used as the basis for variations in compositions with repeating harmonies. Bergamo was also home to the peasant character type of the Zanni from the commedia dell'arte. These roles were usually performed by the shrewd Brighella and the frequently outwitted Harlequin. Relevant for Verlaine is the distinctive costume of these characters, which included a mask with a long nose. This was the same mask beneath which Verlaine caught a glimpse of the Zannis' sadness at being constantly made fun of and exploited by the other characters of their troupe. "Even as they sing in the minor mode of conquering love and the good life," he wrote in his "Clair de Lune," "they do not seem to believe in their happiness, and their song mingles with the moonlight, with the calm moonlight sad and beautiful"[4] (figure 3.3).

Fauré, when he called on Verlaine to explain his music, did so through the image of masked actors "playing the lute and dancing and almost sad beneath their fanciful disguises."[5]

Votre âme est un paysage choisi
Que vont charmant masques et bergamasques
Jouant du luth et dansant et quasi
Tristes sous leurs déguisements fantasques.

Tout en chantant sur le mode mineur
L'amour vainqueur et la vie opportune,
Ils n'ont pas l'air de croire à leur bonheur
Et leur chanson se mêle au clair de lune,

Au calme clair de lune triste et beau,
Qui fait rêver les oiseaux dans les arbres
Et sangloter d'extase les jets d'eau,
Les grands jets d'eau sveltes parmi les marbres.

Your soul is a choice landscape
Where charming maskers and bergamaskers pass
Playing the lute and dancing and almost
Sad beneath their fanciful disguises [masks]

Even as they sing in the minor mode
Of conquering love and the good life
They do not seem to believe in their happiness
And their song mingles with the moonlight,

With the calm moonlight sad and beautiful,
Which makes the birds dream in the trees
And the fountains sob with ecstasy,
The tall slender fountains among the marbles.

FIGURE 3.3   Verlaine, "Clair de Lune" (*Fêtes galantes*).

As we shall see in the next chapter, what is merely a hint in Watteau becomes a palpable feeling in Verlaine, where the term *bergamasque* invokes a fleeting vision of happiness tinged with sadness. It enhances the dreaminess of his imagery by shifting the poem to a distant time and place, where musicians play antiquated instruments and actors dance an old folk dance.

The French philosopher Vladimir Jankélévitch picked up on Verlaine's deliberate use of *bergamasque* to evoke a sense of ambiguity characteristic of the realm of the otherworldly.

Jankélévitch underscores a similar transition through his use of this term to define the music of Fauré: "Like the penumbra, it [bergamasque] involves a particular mélange of light and mystery."[6] In this way, Jankélévitch compares the evanescent charm of Fauré's music with Verlaine's longing to transfix the quality of twilight that casts a magical shadow over several of Watteau's tableaux. Throughout his writings on Fauré, Jankélévitch draws attention to the transcendental quality of his music, describing the Requiem, in particular, as "authentically 'bergamasque,' and not resembling anything else on earth."[7] However hyperbolic they might seem, these remarks offer an excellent starting point for engaging with Debussy's Clair de Lune, a piece that is quintessential *bergamasque*, as we will now see.

CHAPTER 4

POETRY, ART,
AND MUSIC

D EBUSSY'S DECISION TO BORROW the title for his composition from the interlinked eighth and ninth lines of Verlaine's "Clair de Lune" creates a strong alliance between his music and the poem. Set against the backdrop of elegant marble statues and sobbing fountains, Verlaine's lingering imagery of dreaming birds and masked actors dancing and singing in the sad moonlight certainly imbues the atmosphere of Debussy's music. However, it is not only to poetry that we should look in grasping the nuances of the pianistic Clair de Lune. This chapter opens with a consideration of painting, specifically the *fêtes galantes* canvases of Jean-Antoine Watteau (1684–1721), whose sensuous depictions of aristocrats at play mesmerized creative figures of the nineteenth century through their offering of "a magical source of evasion into a dream world of grace and beauty," as described by Maxine Cutler.[1] This chapter proposes that the decorative tableaux created by the painter are behind the efforts of both Verlaine and Debussy to intensify a particular mode of nocturnal beauty in their respective evocations of moonlight.

The trinity of Watteau-Verlaine-Debussy forms an intriguing pyramid. Although he was well regarded during his lifetime, Watteau acquired even greater fame following his rediscovery by two contrasting sections of French society: conservatives who were nostalgic for the splendor of the ancien régime on the one hand and bohemian painters and writers who craved the carefree spirit that pervaded his sensuous paintings on the other.[2] Together, these distinct social groups ensured that Watteau's star continued to shine during the first decades of the nineteenth century. Significant here is how the Romantic mantra "Art for art's sake" took inspiration from Watteau's work. Those who chanted this phrase during the 1830s—the poets and novelists Théophile Gautier, Gérard de Nerval, Victor Hugo, and Arsène Houssaye among them—recognized an aesthetic kinship with the sliver of melancholy that ran through Watteau's paintings.[3] The Goncourt brothers, Edmond and Jules, took this idolatry to a new level in their wistful multivolume celebration of the eighteenth century first published in 1859, *L'art du dix-huitième siècle*.

The brothers' opening article on Watteau referred to many of the associations that had been floating around the painter over the previous few decades.[4] Beginning with a tribute, "The great poet of the eighteenth century is Watteau," this article elevates the status of the painter, thereby ensuring his preeminence within literary circles, one that gave writers even more reason to adore and emulate him. Furthermore, the Goncourts' perception of "a musical and sweetly contagious sadness that runs through the *fêtes galantes*" strengthened prevailing reception of the painter's work in terms of its covert allusions to the state of melancholy.[5] By placing Watteau's paintings in proximity to the sublime realm of music, the brothers secured his place atop the pedestal on which he rested for quite some time. The opening phrase of Verlaine's "Art poétique"— "Music, above all else"—reminds us that a comparison with music was the ultimate compliment in the middle of the nineteenth century. It was not unusual for musicians to reciprocate the gesture; thus, music critics writing well into the early twentieth century would often compare the compositions of Debussy and Gabriel Fauré with Watteau's most celebrated painting, *L'Embarquement pour Cythère* (1717).[6] Even the composer Erik Satie, who was not one to follow trends, acknowledged Watteau in "Le Carnaval" (*Sports et Divertissements*, 1914) through mention of "a melancholic mask." As we saw in the previous chapter, Fauré continued to draw inspiration from Watteau after the First World War, as heard in the music for his Verlaine-inspired divertissement *Masques et Bergamasques* (1919), which he described as being of an "evocative and melancholy—even slightly nostalgic—character."[7]

In keeping with poetic practice of the time, Verlaine's first version of "Clair de Lune," as published on February 20, 1867, in *La Gazette rimée*, credited the source of his inspiration in the line "Au calme clair de lune de Watteau" (in the calm moonlight of Watteau).[8] Although direct mention of Watteau was fairly commonplace among poets, Anatole France, a writer of considerable stature, asked Verlaine where he had seen moonlight painted by Watteau, making the point that Watteau was "le peintre ensoleillé" (the painter bathed in sunlight).[9] In keeping with France, many poets alluded to Watteau's fantastical parkscapes through mention of Cythera, the mythical island blessed by the birth of the goddess of love, Aphrodite. Verlaine, however, took his cue from those less inclined toward the sun, like Albert Glatigny, whose poem "L'attente" (1860) begins "O Cythère mélancolique." In replacing "de Watteau" with "triste et beau" (sad and beautiful), Verlaine removed the explicit reference to Watteau but left an even stronger imprint of the painter's presence in the poem. Verlaine's approach mirrored what Gautier had done in his "Clair de Lune sentimental" where imagery of fountains in the moonlight is bathed in feelings of regret and nostalgia (Variations sur le Carnaval de Venise, *Émaux et camées*, 1852) or Baudelaire in his synesthetic "Harmonie du soir," where sound and scent dance a "melancholic waltz" under a sad and beautiful sky (*Les Fleurs du Mal*).

To be clear, Verlaine and Debussy did not aim to recreate Watteau's dreamy canvases of aristocratic romance and his passion for theatrical comedy. Although Watteau refrained from painting moonlight, what he did hint at through the placement of flirting couples under the shadows of trees, as seen in *La Conversation* and *La Perspective,* was the alluring quality of twilight, a state of transition that fascinated Verlaine as well as Debussy. Alfred Carter explains that while Verlaine retained the lighting and decor of Watteau's art, "the poems are nostalgic and internal . . . the world of the poems is Verlaine's own," a point also affirmed by Cutler in her comparison of Verlaine's poetry with the contemporaneous movements of Impressionism and Symbolism. "Verlaine establishes the keynotes of an atmosphere, perhaps implicit in Watteau, but made explicit in the impressionist interpretation of the Goncourts," she writes. " 'Clair de lune' . . . organizes the symbolism through which Verlaine will define his private universe. . . . Verlaine creates a symbolic portrait of his love in the subtle art of Watteau."[10] The transition into moonlight from twilight marks a retreat from Watteau and a step into the landscapes of the Romantics, for whom the moon had become synonymous with melancholy, the primary association carried through by Debussy's Clair de Lune today. Despite the many artistic visions of the moon that might have shaped Verlaine's and Debussy's conceptions, Watteau's art is especially significant.

A particularly notable comparison between Debussy and Fauré sets the tone for this discussion. In his book *Debussy et le Mystère*, the philosopher Vladimir Jankélévitch describes the music of Fauré as soaring "towards the clouds by ascent and sublimation of the sensory," while Debussy's, particularly the falling arabesques that characterize his *Syrinx* and the *Fêtes galantes* songs, "lead[s] us into the mortal depths of desire and oblivion."[11] The dichotomy between lightness and darkness is one that intrigued Debussy in terms of its structural fluidity, as seen in *Pelléas et Mélisande*. This contrast also appealed to the composer in part for its melding of joy with sadness to form the bittersweet melancholy that nineteenth-century spectators were eager to celebrate in Watteau's work and which they understood as being embraced by the term *bergamasque*.

Watteau did not explicitly paint the moon, but he did hint at its presence in *Pierrot* (1718–19), a painting well known to the Romantics, and one whose melancholic aura they sought to project onto the figure of Watteau himself (figure 4.1). The large, moon-shaped countenance of the clown placed high in the sky is suggestive in this regard, as are Pierrot's white clothes whose billowy, satin-like fabric evokes the shimmery aura of the moon. Pamela Whedon explains how "light reflects from his costume," an effect that Watteau also explored in an earlier painting, *Pierrot Content,* where the figure of Pierrot appears almost luminescent against the twilight setting.[12] Pierre Rosenberg notes the effect of twilight in another early depiction of Pierrot, *La Partie Quarrée,* where "the last rays of light make the silks and satins sparkle."[13]

Even though Pierrot is seen socializing in *Pierrot Content* and *La Partie Quarrée,* scholars have discussed the feelings of isolation and sadness that are foregrounded in *Pierrot.* Ken Ireland draws attention to qualities of pathos, impassiveness, discomfort, and dejection, while Rosenberg notes how Pierrot is "cut off from the world surrounding him, without movement, isolated and alone," a feeling that Martin Green also highlights in his discussion of how performances of the commedia dell'arte in France—the Italian comedy troupe of which Pierrot was a part—portrayed a sense of isolation from the Italians' homeland.[14]

Like the Mona Lisa's mysterious smile, the ambiguous expression that is offered to us in *Pierrot* holds the gaze as our eyes penetrate its surface, looking for clues as to how the clown is feeling and what he might be thinking as he stands at

FIGURE 4.1   Jean-Antoine Watteau, *Pierrot* (ca. 1718–19). Oil on canvas,
184.5 cm × 149.5 cm. Erich Lessing/Art Resource, New York.
Artwork in the public domain.

a distance from the company of his troupe and their donkey.
Following Watteau, the figure who humanized Pierrot more
than any poet or painter was the mime artist Jean-Gaspard
Deburau. Renowned for his mute performances of Pierrot,

Deburau played this role for much of his career, spanning 1816 to 1846.[15] Deburau's modifications and updates to this familiar character were in line with Watteau's *Pierrot*; the clown's isolation from his troupe as seen in this painting was mirrored in Pierrot's (Deburau's) deliberate detachment from the dramatic action. Although Deburau replaced the oversized straw hat of Watteau's *Pierrot* with a snug, black skullcap, his white makeup and white costume—described by the poet Théodore de Banville as being of an epic whiteness—concretized the link between Pierrot and the moon, which Banville further reified in his poem "Pierrot" (*Les Cariatides*, 1842). Here, the misery of the love-struck Pierrot is literally spotlighted by the moon as its beams fall directly on Deburau: "And meanwhile, mysterious and shiny, making him its dearest delight, the white moon with the horns of a bull casts a glance offstage at his friend, Jean Gaspard Deburau."

Banville picked up on Deburau's moonlike appearance and secured the association of Pierrot with the moon in the *Odes funambulesques* (1857), a series of short verses named after the Théâtre des Funambules, where Deburau performed. These writings are introduced through an engraving by Félix Bracquemond based on a design by Charles Voillemot. Here, the violin-playing Pierrot invokes Watteau through a direct, penetrating stare at the audience. At the same time, Bracquemond signals Deburau's distance from *Pierrot* by replacing the straw hat with a trim skullcap. Where the oversized straw cap served to radiate the warm, luminescent light of Pierrot's moonlike face in Watteau's paintings, Bracquemond's image emphasizes Deburau's matte white makeup, brought into focus through removal of the hat, which now sits beside Pierrot while he plays and gazes outward beyond the dance of the cherubs and satyrs. Even as Watteau's scenery adorns many of the poems in this set, Banville renders the association between Pierrot and the moon explicit in "Les Follies-Nouvelles," describing him as "my dear friend Pierrot, cousin of the moon"[16] (figure 4.2).

FIGURE 4.2 Félix Bracquemond, *Frontispice pour les Odes funambulesques* by *Théodore de Banville* (1857). Ink on paper, etching, 3⅜ × 2⅜ in. The Miriam and Ira D. Wallach Division of Art, Prints and Photographs: Print Collection, The New York Public Library. New York Public Library Digital Collections.

There is no Pierrot in Debussy's Clair de Lune, yet this figure's indelible association with the moon and feelings of heartbreak and loneliness by the turn of the twentieth century might have us wondering whether Debussy and Verlaine sketched his presence in the shadows, "under the trees of the great Watteau," as Glatigny put it in his poem "L'attente." In each Clair de Lune, as we shall see, the moon comes to stand in for Pierrot—for his luminescent clothing, as well as for the feeling of seclusion that lurks behind the whiteness of a seemingly vacant stare.

Between the reeds, the big water lilies shone sadly on the calm waters.

Paul Verlaine, "Promenade Sentimentale"

As discussed in chapter 3, it is likely that Debussy's Clair de Lune either took the place of or replaced the title of a piece originally called "Promenade Sentimentale." This latter title leads us to consider two additional poems whose imagery and sentiments likely stirred Debussy's imagination. It is possible that when Debussy first started to sketch the *Suite Bergamasque,* Verlaine's "Promenade Sentimentale," an early poem, spoke to him directly through its visceral portrayal of themes of loneliness and anguish; in the poem, the fading light and warmth of the setting sun brings into focus the eerie qualities of the night in the form of ghoulish mist and stifling shadows that intensify the protagonist's pain and sense of isolation. In switching the title of his piece to Clair de Lune, Debussy indicated a preference for a marvelously dreamy Watteauesque nocturnal landscape, whose subtle interplay between elements of fantasy and reality offers a means of escape from the raw pain that haunts "Promenade" in the manner of Baudelaire. Another relevant source Debussy discovered in the years preceding the *Suite Bergamasque* is Paul Bourget's "Paysage sentimental" (*Les Aveux*, 1882), where reflection on a state of melancholic happiness prolongs the wistful song and dance of Verlaine's masked comedy troupe, and whose emphasis on an isolated yet joyous soul also evokes the opening lines of Clair de Lune. Bourget's comparison of the soul with an aspect of nature—"the pond that grew pale at the bottom of the pale valley"—aligns the interior with the exterior in a way that recalls Baudelaire's exploration of the soul as a landscape in a number of his poems, including "Le mauvais moine" and "Le voyage."[17] In contrast, Verlaine's personification of landscape in the opening line of "Clair de Lune" invokes the realm of fantasy as fanciful images populate the scene and bring it to life.

As we have seen, Debussy turned his attention to the *Suite Bergamasque* around 1890, eight years after he had first set Verlaine's "Clair de Lune" as a song while a student at the Paris Conservatoire. We can only speculate on the reasons why Debussy composed another setting nine years later: the first song of his *Fêtes galantes* (1891). Was it a feeling of dissatisfaction with his 1882 version after hearing Fauré's setting of the same poem in 1887? Or was it perhaps his continuing fascination with the way in which Verlaine mingles emotion, sound, and imaginary bodies through the filter of moonlight?

Given Debussy's youth and eagerness to learn, this decade in particular saw a tremendous growth in terms of his compositional maturity. The musicologist Roger Nichols has described Debussy's inability to integrate a recurring rhythmic figure in the first setting as disturbing "the atmos-phere of the accompaniment" through its failure to create unity. In contrast, Nichols regards the subtle integration of a rhythmic motif in the second setting as successful.[18] Nichols also compares Debussy's approach to text setting (tending to-ward repetition in the first, but not in the second), phrasing (constrained in the first, but more fluid in the second), me-lodic development and texture (more varied in the second than the first), and harmony (more conventional in the first than the second) as indicating the various ways in which Debussy was maturing as a composer of songs.[19]

Alongside thinking about these songs from a teleolog-ical perspective that favors mature craftsmanship over youthful experimentation, we might also consider them as a pair, where the youthful exuberance of the first is reflected in Debussy's quintessentially Romantic interpretation of Verlaine, while the subdued languor of the second reflects a more introspective engagement with the poem. The joyous mood of the first song is reflected in the dance-like articula-tion of a triple-time meter (3/8) and its accentuation through the brightness of F♯ major, where the high A♯ rings with a striking brilliance in the soprano tessitura as she underscores the happy mood at "la vie opportune" (the good life) and with the alteration of the opening melody at the reprise ("Au calme clair de lune"—with the calm moonlight). (Listen to audio example 4.1 ▶.)[20] There are obvious rhythmic and mo-tivic allusions to the musical style of the French composer Jules Massenet in these moments, which encapsulate the sense of joie de vivre that runs through the genre of the *fêtes galantes*. Significantly, tonal emphasis on the Neapolitan key area, G major, is brought out through meandering melodic motion at "leur chanson se mêle au clair de lune" ("their song mingles with the moonlight"), the decorative undulation of which pays tribute to nineteenth-century operatic exoticism.

Just as this song seems to exoticize the sunshine and laughter of Watteau's *L'Embarquement*—perhaps indicative of Debussy's burgeoning affair with Marie-Blanche Vasnier—his second setting of Verlaine's text invites us to appreciate a *fête galante* scene at twilight. (Listen to audio example 4.2 ⊙.)[21] In contrast to the clichéd augmented seconds of the first song, Debussy here offers a more probing engagement with the exotic as heard in the pentatonic formulation of distinct rhythmic layers, no doubt inspired by the timbres of the Javanese gamelan music he had just heard at the Paris World's Fair of 1889. The underlying hint of *tristesse*, or sadness, comes through in the "moonlight atmosphere of the accompaniment" (as noted by Léon Vallas), where sixteenth-note patterning accompanies languorous vocal phrases, initially reluctant to move away from D♯.[22] The dance-like characterization of the first Clair de Lune contrasts with the indolent feel of this song, which slowly becomes more agitated with the arrival of the second stanza: "Tout en chantant sur le mode mineur" ("Even as they sing in the minor mode"). Although there are many more ways in which the two songs differ, a fleeting motif that emerges with an uncanny insistence in the middle voice of the final measures of the second plants a seed in the listener's mind (E♯–D♯). This motif allows us to connect the dreamy vision of this scene with that of the first song through the transformation of the interval of an augmented second in the first (D–E♯) into a major second in the second song (E♯–D♯) (example 4.1).

Returning to the pianistic Clair de Lune, it is worth nothing that these two songs, when viewed as a pair, reveal Debussy's appreciation for the dualities that characterize the genre of the *fêtes galantes*—lightness and darkness, dream and reality, happiness and sadness. As explored in chapter 3, these oppositions are specifically captured by the term *bergamasque*, a term that the Goncourt brothers also used to invoke opposition; the "bergamasque laughter" of Watteau's work is joyful and sad in the same instance.[23] Also relevant in this regard is Fauré's "Clair de Lune," which provides a fitting point of mediation between the Debussy songs in two ways: chronologically, Fauré's song appears at the halfway point in 1887, and musically, its lack of concern for Verlaine's imagery—Jankélévitch describes this song as being "indifferent to the visual suggestions of the text"—opens up the potential for musical reimagination beyond the realm of song.[24] I have already proposed that Fauré's song lent its subtitle and motivic gestures to the second movement of the *Suite Bergamasque*, the Menuet. As proposed by the pianist Graham Johnson, could it be that Fauré's "inspired idea to make of [his song] a piano piece with a vocal obbligato" was the catalyst for Debussy's own decision to compose an instrumental work based on Verlaine's poem?[25]

It is certainly satisfying to think of Fauré's ironic reading of Verlaine as nudging Debussy toward a pianistic treatment of Clair de Lune. To this end, Fauré's unravelling piano and vocal parts, with their penchant for soloistic expression, might have played a role in revealing the potential for engagement with Verlaine through purely instrumental means. Also significant in this regard is the fortuitous delineation of a B♭ major harmony in the piano at the moment the voice recalls songs that "they sing in the minor mode." The shifting major-minor landscape of Debussy's piano opening seems to pick up from the playful contradiction of this moment in Fauré's song; without the burden of words, maybe Debussy believed he could capture that elusive *bergamasque* laughter heard by the Goncourts.

Debussy was already moving in this direction in the *Petite Suite* (1889), a piano composition for four hands, where titles for two of the movements are taken from Verlaine's *Fêtes galantes* poems "En bateau" and "Cortège."[26] Verlaine's "En bateau" prolongs the romantic mood of the opening poem from his *Fêtes galantes* set, the "Clair de Lune": reflections of a starry, moonlit night shimmer in the water as strains of plucked music accompany amorous indiscretions and whispered longings between lovers.

Musically, too, Debussy establishes a number of subtle connections between this nocturnal scene and that of his Clair de Lune for piano. Both pieces are set in a compound meter: En bateau in 6/8 and Clair de Lune in 9/8. The melodic material of these pieces is also treated in a similar way: after a first presentation, the opening phrase is immediately repeated before the music veers in a new direction. Also similar is the emphasis on streams of rising and falling parallel thirds, as well as the rhythmic character of the works; Debussy's use of ties between notes creates a nice rhythmic lilt, which is complemented in the alternation between duple and triple groupings. The left hand's accompaniment of En bateau seems to flow directly into the *un poco mosso* of Clair de Lune, given how each arpeggiation stays strictly within a two-octave limit. These kinds of interconnections help us to hear Clair de Lune as an early exploration of the topic of the *fêtes galantes* in an instrumental genre. Even though Clair de Lune was published in 1905, the restrained virtuosity of the piano writing in comparison with *L'isle joyeuse* (1904), another *fête galante* work, is indicative of its status as an early piece within Debussy's oeuvre.

FINDING THE "BLUE NOTE"

A number of correlations become noticeable when considering the poem in relation to the music. Most obvious is the overlap between the three-stanza form of Verlaine's text and the ternary structure of Debussy's composition: the *un poco mosso* corresponds with Verlaine's second stanza, where Debussy's emphasis on a major sonority recalls

Fauré's playful interpretation of Verlaine's "minor mode," as well as the *a tempo I* with the final verse. Equally significant is Debussy's effort to capture the narrative trajectory of the poem through gesture and register: with Verlaine, we sense a progression from the human pursuits of dance and music making to the magical realm of dreaming birds and sobbing fountains bathed in moonlight. It is the repetition of the phrase "clair de lune" in the ninth line that enables the transition from the earthly to the ethereal, where Verlaine subtly changes the quality of moonlight to one imbued with calmness, sadness, and beauty as we cross the threshold. Debussy signals a similar shift through the upward registral motion of his final section (marked *morendo jusqu'à la fin* in the score: dying away until the end) where a repeating C♭–D♭ motif slowly climbs toward a resplendent high A♭. Just as Verlaine lifts our gaze upward toward the tall fountains and the moon, Debussy seems to guide our ear similarly. This A♭ is not the highest pitch of the piece, but it feels high because of the slow climb, with the persistent C♭ refusing to fall to B♭ as we might expect or to A♭ as it had done in the *un poco mosso*, where the C♭ provided a modal hue (example 4.2).

Debussy adds tonal color through the use of this dissonant C♭, but he also draws on this pitch to (again) plant a seed in the listener's mind, since C♭ later performs a transformative role equivalent to Verlaine's repetition of the "clair de lune" phrase. When this pitch sounds in the final section, it seems to come out of nowhere, its subtle, accented intrusion in the left hand at measure 59 occurring when the opening theme is repeated. It is significant that Debussy doesn't introduce the C♭ with the first return of the opening melody at the *a*

EXAMPLE 4.2   A repeating C♭–D♭ motif climbs towards a resplendent high A♭.

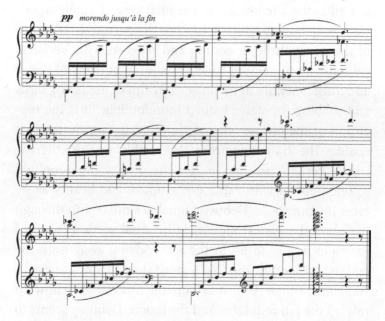

tempo I (m. 51); in releasing it gently into the musical texture with the second statement instead, he follows Verlaine's pattern of repetition, where the second iteration of "clair de lune" is more nuanced than the first. The C♭ of measure 59 is thus imbued with calmness, sadness, and beauty. The pianist Maurice Dumesnil recalled how Debussy wanted this note to "be brought out, thus emphasizing the change of color."[27] (example 4.3)

Following the French writer George Sand, we might call this the "note bleue" (blue note) in Debussy's work. Of Chopin's improvisations, Sand once said, "The 'note bleue' resonates and there we are, in the azure of the transparent night."[28] Like Chopin's blue note, Debussy's also transports

EXAMPLE 4.3   Debussy's C♭, the "note bleue."

his listeners into a scene of nocturnal enchantment, but with a Verlaine-like twist: the little nudge of the C♭ as suggested, through its sparing but deliberate placements, allows it to linger, to work its way slowly into our consciousness until we realize that the music we're hearing is not the same as that of the opening. The playfulness of masked actors is now tainted with a memory whose truth can only be perceived in nature, through light and water. In this way, the modal inflection provided by each C♭ realizes the feeling of longing and regret that holds the poem and music in delicate balance.

The upward motion of the C♭–D♭ motif at the end is worth noting, since it goes against Debussy's usual tendency to write melodies that rise and fall in an arch-like contour, that is, arabesque melodies. Inspired by the visual designs of art nouveau, melodic arabesques feature a long, undulating line, reflected here in the meandering melody that slowly unravels through three octaves from measures 1 to 9. Having reached the lower register, the melody immediately bounces back up to initiate a similar descent. The fluid motion of the melody owes partly to shifts between triplet and duple rhythms, which give a nice sense of ebb and flow throughout the piece. A lack of metric emphasis on the downbeat supplements the rhythmic suppleness of the melody by projecting a sense of meter that feels quite free. As seen in his letters and writings, Debussy had great admiration for this kind of melodic shape, going so far as to credit it with the evocation of beauty and expression, particularly in the music of Palestrina, Orlando di Lasso, and J. S. Bach.[29] (see example 4.4)

We hear this kind of melody throughout Debussy's oeuvre. In his piano works, however, it often creates a point of contrast against textures that favor block chords—as heard in the *tempo rubato*—as well as those that exhibit intricate figuration or an undulating accompaniment and melody—as heard at the *un poco mosso* and *calmato* sections. Debussy's notion of form was not tied to a traditional preoccupation with melody and harmony. As seen in Clair de Lune, his piano pieces were often structured according to the principle of creating distinct textures and moods within a single piece. This musical preference explains why many of his

EXAMPLE 4.4   Arabesque melody in Clair de Lune.

contemporaries spoke of his approach to composing and playing the piano as being orchestral, with each section seeming to take on its own scoring. Early orchestrators of this piece may have heard the opening, with its long phrases and legato streams of closely spaced thirds and sustained chords, as being well-suited to the woodwinds, while the declamatory quality of the *tempo rubato* invites the warm timbre of unison strings. The *un poco mosso* seems to call for a harp in its undulating arpeggiation and a woodwind instrument such as the oboe to play the legato, sustained melody on top (as Debussy advised Dumesnil, "The left hand arpeggios should be fluid, mellow, drowned in pedal, as if played by a harp on a background of strings").[30] A contrapuntal texture at the *calmato* could be well delivered by the strings, the cellos and basses holding the A♭–E♭ pedal while the upper strings pass around melodic motifs. The final section demands the entire orchestra, given the richness of the harmonies and diversity of musical gesture ranging from arpeggiation to sustained melody and full chords. Debussy's cultivation of contrasting textures is central to the wide appeal of Clair de Lune, since musicians might extract any part of the piece as the basis for reinterpretation without fearing a loss of coherence (as we saw in chapter 2). In this respect, Debussy's treatment of harmony, with its slow-paced rate of change, ensures a sense of continuity even as the textural character of each section remains distinct.

The charm of Debussy's harmonic palette in Clair de Lune derives from his ease of transition between major and minor sonorities, such that the tonal identity of a passage is often in flux. The subtle voice leading of the opening is especially effective in this regard, its shifts between diminished, dominant seventh, and inverted chords serving to introduce the flavor of the *bergamasque*, with its allusions to feelings of joy laced with sadness. From the outset, Debussy encourages the listener to enter the realm of dream by manipulating his or her expectations of musical convention. As with the elimination of metrical emphasis on the downbeat at the beginning, Debussy enhances the floating quality of the opening phrase by avoiding articulation of the tonic D♭ major. The first measure of the piece similarly leaves the listener guessing as to whether the piece is in F minor, as suggested by the opening minor third, or D♭ major, as answered by the entrance of D♭ at the end of the measure. As we have seen with his treatment of C♭, Debussy enjoys playing with the listener's memory. Thus, even as he resolves the tonal dilemma by offering a perfect cadence in D♭ major (mm. 8–9), his hushed F minor coloring of the melody at its return in measure 51 (played pianississimo) has the listener briefly wondering again which is really the home key.

The changing shades of Debussy's harmonies have the important role of maintaining variety, given his tendency to privilege repetition in the melody. Thus, when he repeats the opening phrase from measure 9, he subtly changes its harmonization. Whereas the melody is supported by a diminished seventh chord in measure 2, its re-harmonization in measure 10 is ensured by the subdominant, G♭ major. Debussy does not undertake exact repetition. As the textural writing in this opening section shifts from legato voice leading to a more chordal style of accompaniment, the melody also undergoes subtle variation during its repetition, which calls for different harmonic expression. For example, the resolution of a dominant seventh in measure 13 into a B♭ minor chord in the following bar facilitates a transition into the *tempo rubato* section, whose minor hues quickly give way to D♭ major for the middle section, *un poco mosso*.

If one particular place in Clair de Lune signals what is to come in Debussy's piano compositions of the future, it is in this section, the *un poco mosso*. Here, his tonal writing exhibits characteristic *bergamasque* charm through its momentary slips onto a parallel minor seventh sonority, whose A♭ and C♭ undergo an ingenious enharmonic shift in measure 36 to G♯ and B♮, thereby enabling a seamless transition to the brighter key of E major for the most virtuosic section of the piece, *En animant*. The arpeggio figuration that opens the *un poco mosso* assumes a greater vivacity here, and, together with that of the *calmato* section, this sixteenth-note patterning looks ahead to the kind of ornamental writing that would come to be associated with the topic of water in such pieces as Reflets dans l'eau (*Images*, 1905) and Poissons d'or (*Images*, 1907).

CLAIR DE LUNE AT THE PIANO

Although Debussy did not make a recording of Clair de Lune, we can hear him playing many of his other compositions on the Gramophone audio disc recordings of 1904 and the Welte-Mignon reproducing piano rolls of 1912. As exciting as it is to hear Debussy play, these audio sources must be approached with a degree of caution, since they do not give an accurate picture of Debussy's playing style. Roy Howat reminds us that each of these early recording technologies had its own different limitations and thus ran the risk of misrepresenting certain aspects of performance, especially with a pianist who performed with as much subtlety as Debussy. About piano rolls (which essentially record whether each key and pedal is up or down at any given moment) Howat explains, "A pianist who played with a very decisive touch and pedalling can be well reproduced without much difficulty. . . . However, what if a pianist's touch plays with subtle half-tints, half-pedalling, and all sorts of voicings within parts and chords[?] . . . This was the sort of playing for which Debussy was remembered."[31] Given that memory can also distort the past, as seen in the small inconsistencies between one recollection and another, the handful of reminiscences selected here are those that intersect most closely with the personal side of Debussy as glimpsed in his letters and writings.

Today, performances of Clair de Lune on the piano tend to favor an elastic tempo and generous use of rubato in the broad sense of free rhythmic treatment. It might be surprising to learn that Debussy was often strict when it came to matters of tempo, as recalled by singers and pianists who worked with him.[32] Dumesnil remembers Debussy complaining about his triplets as being out of time in Hommage à Rameau (*Images*, 1905), while those in Clair de Lune Debussy found too strictly *in* time. As with the performance of dynamics and tempo rubato, Debussy seemed to favor a more shaded progression of events. Dumesnil recalls Debussy's reaction to his performance of a passage from Clair de Lune: "You exaggerate both the crescendo and the rubato. The latter must be done within the entire phrase, never on a single beat."[33] In the relevant passage, from measure 15, Debussy's expressive markings make his expectations clear: *peu à peu crescendo et animé* ("become louder and faster little by little").

In the earliest recording we have of Clair de Lune from 1918, the pianist Benno Moiseiwitsch offers an almost melodramatic shaping of this phrase, coming dangerously close to "a climax à la Mascagni or Leoncavallo," which Debussy had asked Dumesnil to avoid. (Listen to audio example 4.3 ▶.)[34] The subsequent tempo change to *un poco mosso* is also interpreted rather liberally by Moiseiwitsch, who takes off in this section, his left hand arpeggiation sounding rather bravura beneath the sonorous thirds and sixths of the right hand melody, which he nonetheless gathers together into a beautifully sculpted phrase. Such an animated tempo at measure 27 means he has to create even more movement at the *En animant* of bar 37.

The British pianist Harold Bauer created a completely different sense of pacing at the same moment. (Listen to audio example 4.4 ▶.) In his recording of 1929, Bauer treated measure 19, at the moment where Debussy indicates *peu à peu crescendo et animé*, as the climactic point of the phrase begun in bar 15.[35] The subsequent (mildly altered) repetition of measures 19–20 in bars 21–22 sounds more like an echo, while the next, slower—and not at all *animé*—iteration (mm. 23–24) marks a soft retreat into the arpeggiated chords that close the section. The music seems to fade away toward the undulating arpeggiations of the *un poco mosso*. Meanwhile, in his 1933 recording, Bauer's student the American pianist George Copeland seems to come the closest to Debussy's expressive markings at this spot, even though the accelerated pace of his *En animant* outdoes that of Moiseiwitsch. (Listen to audio example 4.5 ⓓ.)[36] Interestingly, Copeland seems to make an about-face in a later recording from 1963, where he offers an altogether brisk reading of the piece; the tempo is faster and the phrasing less indulgently dreamy, changes that seem to recall Debussy's comment "I don't feel music the same way every day."[37]

Unlike Moiseiwitsch, Bauer and Copeland received coaching from Debussy, the latter reportedly quite intensively over a few months in 1910. Copeland's somewhat literal reading of the music in the 1963 recording reminds us of the care Debussy took to annotate his scores and the diligence with which he expected pianists to follow his markings in cultivating a natural style of playing. An early biographer, Louis Laloy, provides an especially compelling assessment of the composer's approach to writing for the piano, noting, "When the performer has sensed what is there, he must not exert himself to put in what is not there, and particularly not 'effects.'" In discussing the mood of the piece, Laloy warns against the pursuit of affect: "It would be better to mistake completely the spirit of a piece . . . than abruptly to break the spell with a jab or a grimace."[38] Laloy's critique of a frequent error by pianists might still ring true today: "Pianists must give up the presumption of 'bringing out the tune,'" he wrote, before clarifying: "When thoroughly understood, the melody will take on by itself the slight prominence which is needed; to insist would be to fall into Romantic affectation." In this way, Laloy calls attention to the textural nuances of Debussy's music, where gestures are not organized along a line of hierarchy that highlights melody and virtuosity. Speaking about decorative figurations, Laloy explains: "It would be better to blur these patterns . . . than to overcome the difficulties they present in a triumphant manner," a comment that reminds us of Debussy's criticism of Ricardo Viñes's dry playing.[39]

Laloy's emphasis on tone, especially the "transparent sonority . . . achieved by a clean and never harsh attack," calls attention to the unique sound Debussy elicited from the piano in his own playing, as noted by several of his contemporaries.[40] In tandem with Laloy, who asked the pianist to "feel the sound in his fingertips" while maintaining "softness in strength, and strength in softness," the pianist Yvonne Lefébure recalled Debussy's playing as massaging the piano keys, "with a sound that was softly mellow yet powerful and radiant." Her comment is reinforced by Dumesnil's description of "the tone [Debussy] extracted from the Blüthner [piano]. . . . [It] was the loveliest, the most elusive and ethereal I have ever heard. How did he do it? I noticed that at times the position of his fingers, particularly in soft chord passages, was almost flat. He seemed to caress the keys by rubbing them gently downward in an oblique motion instead of pushing them down in a straight line."[41] Louise Liebich also noted Debussy's "soft, deep touch which evoked full, rich, many-shaded sonorities," as did another aristocrat, Debussy's student Madame Gerard de Romilly, who was astonished at how with "rather unusual nails, curved like claws . . . he was able to produce such soft, cushiony sounds."[42] Such was Debussy's penchant for a warm, resonant timbre that he bought a Blüthner boudoir grand piano equipped with a set of aliquot strings designed to maximize its singing power. Dumesnil remembered how Debussy asked him to press both the tre corde and una corda pedals before playing Clair de Lune, "so that the overtones would vibrate immediately upon contact."[43]

The refined, multihued soundscape of Debussy's mature playing seems to be at odds with earlier characterizations of his demeanor at the piano. Gabriel Pierné remembered how as a student Debussy "used to charge at the piano and force all his effects. He seemed to be in a rage with the instrument, rushing up and down it with impulsive gestures and breathing noisily during the difficult bits. These faults gradually receded and occasionally he would obtain effects of an astonishing softness."[44] Descriptions of Debussy's playing often hinged on his ability to lose himself in the depths of his imagination. Léon-Paul Fargue recalled Debussy's improvisations: "He would start by brushing the keys, prodding the odd one here and there, making a pass over them and then he would sink into velvet, sometimes accompanying himself, his head down, in an attractive nasal voice, like a sung whisper. He gave the impression of delivering the piano of its sound, like a mother of her child. He cradled it, sang to it softly, like a rider to his horse, like a shepherd to his flock, like a thresher to his oxen."[45] Debussy's beloved Mary Garden, the Scottish singer who first sang the role of Mélisande, also spoke of his improvisations at the piano as having an otherworldly quality: "At those moments Debussy was in that far-off world of his, inspired, as if in a trance. He just sat there and played. He never moved and he never said a word."[46]

Perhaps because of stage fright, Debussy rarely gave first performances of his piano pieces, that honor most often having been bestowed on the Catalan virtuoso Ricardo Viñes. Among the premieres given by Viñes were those of *Pour le Piano, Estampes, Masques, L'isle joyeuse*, both books of *Images*, and several of the *Préludes*. The absence of mentions of the *Suite Bergamasque* in critical reviews of Viñes's recitals from 1905 suggests he did not introduce Clair de Lune to Parisian audiences; either the suite's long gestation or its delayed publication seems to have resulted in its overshadowing by more recently composed works. Clair de Lune started to feature regularly in the French press after 1907, when Lucien Wurmser included it in a recital at the Salle Pleyel.[47]

Where the *Suite Bergamasque* was premiered remains a mystery. Just as the German American pianist Walter Rummel gave the first known performance of Debussy's Ce qu'a vu le vent d'Ouest (*Préludes*, Book 1) at a concert in Stockbridge, Massachusetts, on July 26, 1910, it is possible that Clair de Lune was first performed by Copeland on April 17, 1906, at a recital in his native city of Boston, just two years after he performed the *Deux Arabesques* there (January 1904).[48] Although some of the claims made by Copeland concerning the closeness of his friendship with Debussy are questionable, Copeland is to be especially credited with championing his music in the States. During the few months of his contact with Debussy in 1910, Debussy coached him on several of his pieces. Furthermore, Copeland went on to record Clair de Lune six times.[49]

Space in this chapter permits me only to point the reader toward a handful of other notable recordings, such as that of Walter Gieseking (the pianist whose playing was considered by Emma Bardac as being the closest to that of her husband, Debussy), who recorded the *Suite Bergamasque* for Columbia in 1931, a year after Marius-François Gaillard recorded the *Suite* for Odéon. Also to be mentioned is the 1924 Victor recording by the Texas pianist Olga Samaroff (née Lucy Hickenlooper), whose warmth and clarity of tone is to be admired, and Leopold Godowsky's recording for Brunswick of 1925, with its exquisite voicing and sustained melody lines.

No matter how many times we have heard Clair de Lune, each of the pianists mentioned here gives us something new, whether a warmth of tone we have never before heard or an unfamiliar fragment of melody that emerges from the murmuring layers of the piece. As we reflect on the unique attributes of each recording, the title of Debussy's composition brings into view the figure of Verlaine, as he looks to Watteau for the backdrop of his poem. Debussy's Clair de Lune not only transposes the imagery and sentiments of the painting and the poem. His composition goes beneath the masks of the actors to capture their elusive sadness and make their sorrow known and felt. Clair de Lune might be commonly perceived as a simple, evocative tone poem, but it is also, as we have seen, one of Debussy's earliest and successful attempts to cultivate atmosphere through sound.

CHAPTER 5

DEBUSSY AND
THE MOON

P AUL VERLAINE'S SAD AND beautiful moon was one of
many lunar portrayals that shaped Debussy's conception of moonlight. Looking beyond and around Verlaine,
this final chapter explores the cultural climate that informed
Debussy's evocation, allowing us to consider the different
manifestations of moonlight that are inflected through his
own Clair de lune. Having analyzed the nuances of Verlaine's
and Debussy's stylistic approaches in the previous chapter,
the broad overview of this chapter encourages us to take
a step back as we continue to trace aesthetic connections
and deepen the knowledge we have gained thus far concerning the alignment of the moon with topics of romance,
dreaming, nostalgia, mystery, and melancholy.

Understood within a wider historical and cultural framework, these associations can be seen to extend from the

literary innovations of Charles Baudelaire, Edgar Allan Poe, Maurice Maeterlinck, and Stéphane Mallarmé, four of the writers who mattered most to Debussy. In reflecting on Verlaine's title "Clair de lune," Debussy may have also had certain musical precedents in mind: songs on the topic of the moon and night by Franz Schubert, Camille Saint-Saëns, and Gabriel Fauré, as well as the opening movement from Ludwig van Beethoven's C♯ minor "Moonlight" Sonata no. 14, op. 27/2, and Vincenzo Bellini's "Casta Diva" from the opera *Norma*, both of which are sustained by repeating arpeggiation, as in Debussy's piece. Visual representations of the night by two of Debussy's favorite painters, J. M. W. Turner and J. A. M. Whistler, are also likely to have played a role in catalyzing his sonic allusions to moonlight, along with depictions of night scenes in Japanese woodblock prints, which he found to be a constant source of delight and inspiration.

My critical cue in writing this chapter comes from the composer Paul Dukas, who captured the creative energy of this time in a way that reveals the multiple stimuli to which Debussy was exposed: "Impressionism, symbolism, and poetic realism, were united in one great contest of enthusiasm, curiosity, and intellectual emotion. All these painters, poets, and sculptors, were engaged in analysing matter . . . their one endeavor being to make words, sounds, colours, and lines express new shades of feelings."[1] Dukas's emphasis on the pursuit of novelty reveals the extent to which experimental approaches to the creation of art encouraged cross-media collaboration and intellectual exchange between musicians, visual artists, and writers. While these same impulses led to critics labeling Debussy an Impressionist composer, his resistance to this title may partly be attributed to the multifaceted nature of his approach to composition. Certainly, a singular alignment with Impressionism runs the risk of obscuring the numerous other influences that shaped his thought and creative practice, not to mention the extent to which his innovations challenged and, to some extent, went beyond the various experimental trends of his day.

A good point of comparison in this regard is (once more) the eighteenth-century painter Jean-Antoine Watteau. The ambivalence surrounding Watteau as a painter of playful scenes filled with laughter and sunlight—as typified in his rose-tinted *L'Embarquement pour Cythère*—as well as those scenes that capture intimate, plaintive whispers exchanged at twilight—*Assemblée dans un parc* (1716–1717), for instance—is relevant to how Debussy's personality and his work are widely understood today. Prompted by critics of his time, some textbooks still align Debussy's music firmly with the sun-drenched movement of Impressionism. At the same time, some others have explored fruitful associations between Debussy's music and the contemporaneous literary movement of Symbolism, especially with regard to the opera *Pelléas et Mélisande* (based on a play by Maeterlinck), and his unfinished operas inspired by Poe's stories *The Fall of the House of Usher* and *The Devil in the Belfry*.[2] Debussy's interest in evoking mystery and his fascination for nocturnal themes suggest an immediate connection with Symbolism, given the recurrence of the moon as a motif in Symbolist literature and drama, but it also invokes Monet's notion of the *enveloppe* as discussed in chapter 1, which was a parallel driving force behind Debussy's suggestion of intense atmospheres through sound. Despite Debussy's aversion to the terms Impressionism and Symbolism, his artistic engagement with Symbolist aesthetics was ultimately responsible for initiating a change in his creative method, a shift whose impact can be measured in how differently he began to treat the moon by the end of the nineteenth century, particularly after his encounter with Maeterlinck.

Although its characterization varies from context to context, the moon, and attendant topics of the night and twinkling stars, features across a variety of genres in Debussy's oeuvre, including songs, *Pelléas et Mélisande*, some piano pieces, and the movements Nuages and Sirènes from the orchestral *Trois Nocturnes*. In these works, the shifting textures and varying expressive functions of the moon indicate the quiet but significant ways in which Debussy's compositional style and aesthetic tastes evolved and diversified. While the moon may be a universal imaginary construct, the attention it received in French cultural life between 1890 and the 1920s offers a unique vantage point for engaging with the artistic currents that informed and followed from Debussy's own contribution in the form of his Clair de Lune.

CHANGING FACES OF THE MOON

Since Debussy was an avid reader of poetry throughout his life, one of the first places we might look for insights into his aesthetic leanings are his songs. The composition of vocal music preoccupied Debussy while he was still a student at the Paris Conservatoire, one of his earliest settings of 1879 taking the "Ballade à la lune" (from *Premières poésies*, 1829–1835) by the satirical Romantic poet Alfred de Musset as its text. Although Debussy's song has been lost, his unusual choice of poetry offers an intimate glimpse into the young composer's sense of humor: "It was, in the dark night, on the yellowed steeple, the moon, like a dot on an *i*. . . . Moon, what dark spirit walks at the end of a leash through the gloom, your face and your profile? Are you the one-eyed heavens' single eye? Which bigoted cherub peers at us beneath your pale mask? Are you merely a ball? A big fat daddy-long-legs that rolls, that rolls without legs and arms?"[3] Debussy's subtle playfulness was long-lasting to the extent that satire and parody were never far from his artistic visions as heard in such pieces as Doctor Gradus ad Parnassum and Golliwogg's Cakewalk from *Children's Corner* (1908), and Minstrels from *Préludes* (Book 1, 1910). With regard to his musical evocations of the moon, these took on a more serious, Romantic glow in his first works.

Unlike the poetry of Musset, to which Debussy turned just three times during these early years, that of Théodore de Banville, a poet identified with the Parnassian school of thought and an important precursor for the Symbolists, preoccupied Debussy more extensively. In his nocturnal-themed poetry, Banville was likely guided by Victor Hugo's mysterious evocations of the moon in the latter's "Clair de Lune" (*Les Orientales*, 1829), "A Virgil" (*Les Voix intérieures*, 1837), and "La fête chez Thérèse" (*Les Contemplations*, 1856), where such characterizations take on a magical hue in the form of a blue moonlight that bathes the horizon. As we have seen, Banville's "Pierrot" (*Les Cariatides*, 1842) reflects his attraction to Watteau's *fêtes galantes* for their rich assemblage of characters drawn from the Italian commedia dell'arte, not to mention the finesse and subtlety with which the painter cultivated the narrative details of each scene. While Banville's portrayal of a sad Pierrot recalls Watteau's own *Pierrot* (see figure 4.1), Debussy's humorous adaptation of the nursery rhyme "Au clair de la lune" in his setting of Banville's poem underscores the clown's unhappy state through the unexpectedly strange (constantly slipping) harmonization of the children's song. (Listen to audio example 5.1 ▶.)[4]

The night returns as a significant character in other poems by Banville, taking on the hue of the *fêtes galantes* in "Arlequin et Colombine" (1853) and "Nuit d'étoiles" (*Les Stalactites*, 1846), as well as in the *comédie héroïque Diane au bois* (1864). Debussy's dramatic treatment of the latter reveals the first signs of his lifelong interest in ancient Greece as a musical topic. In "Nuit d'étoiles," the poignant breeze and fragrance of the starry night fuel melancholy and nostalgia, while *Diane au bois* recalls the myth of Endymion: moonlight adorns the sleeping face of Eros, making him appear even more irresistible to the chaste goddess Diana, who unwillingly falls in love.

The magical takes on the aura of the supernatural in some of Debussy's songs from 1882, such as his setting of Charles Cros's "L'Archet" (from *Le coffret de santal*, 1873), which conjures up the macabre tone of Poe's gothic fantasies. Similarly, Maurice Bouchor's "Le matelot qui tombe à l'eau" offers another Poe-like vision: "There is a singing on the water through the mist; it must be a sailor longing to throw himself into the water for the moon. The moon cleaves the sobbing waves, the sailor falls into the water . . . a few notes drift back across the water."[5] Interestingly, the grotesqueness of this image is entirely missing from the accompaniment, whose intricate pianistic figuration looks ahead to Debussy's later stylized evocations of water. (Listen to audio example 5.2 ⊙.)[6]

Although Debussy was familiar with the poetry of the Symbolists by this time, his own Verlaine-inspired poetry for the song cycle *Proses Lyriques* (1892–1893) prolongs a distinctly Romantic vision of the night. Thus, the moon in "De Rêve" is not white and cold as it often is with Decadent and Symbolist writers, but golden and warm. In this sense, it corresponds with Verlaine's "Tournez, tournez, bons chevaux de bois," where "the velvet sky is slowly clothed in golden stars" (*Romances sans paroles*, 1874), and Mallarmé's "Eventail" (1884), which conjures "the scepter of pink shores stagnant on golden evenings."[7] The warmth and comfort offered by the moon extends to Debussy's poem "De Grève": "But the moon, pitiful to all! Comes by and soothes this gray struggle, and slowly caresses its little friends who offer themselves like loving lips to this warm and white kiss."[8] Despite Debussy's Symbolist approach in setting the text, his literary conception of the moon in the *Proses Lyriques* is still veiled in the Romantic undertones of Baudelaire and early Verlaine.

VERLAINE, BAUDELAIRE, AND A CHANGE OF LIGHTING

Nocturnal themes intertwine the oeuvres of Verlaine and Baudelaire, who both showed an interest in what the scholar of French literature Philip Stephan calls "obscured lighting—night, moonlight, fog, and overcast weather."[9] As with Debussy, visual techniques seem to have influenced their exploration of these themes in poetry. The literary critic James Huneker argued, "Like Whistler, whom he often met . . . [Baudelaire] could not help showing his aversion to 'foolish sunsets.' In a word, Baudelaire, into whose brain had entered too much moonlight, was the father of a lunar school of poetry, criticism and fiction."[10] One might easily place Verlaine as a student in Baudelaire's "lunar school," although the quality of light that he wished to evoke was noticeably different. With regard to Verlaine's visual aesthetic, Stephan notes: "Close attention to the visual effects of obscured lighting suggests . . . the esthetic of Impressionist painters. . . . Verlaine consciously and systematically adapted the principles of French Impressionism to his poetry."[11] In addition, tinges of Symbolist ambiguity in Verlaine's mature writing become especially noticeable when his descriptions of the moon are placed alongside Baudelaire's stark and gritty visions of the night.

As prompted by Turner's paintings of fog and mist, Verlaine's interest in translating painterly vagueness as a poetic ideal is seen in how his presentation of the moon strives to transfix the magical state of twilight, a quality of luminescence that Baudelaire also explored in "Paysage" (*Tableaux Parisiens*, 1861), where "the moon adds its pale enchantment" to his dreams of Paris.[12] As a poetic subject, twilight points to the changing quality of light, mood, and atmosphere as night moves into day—as in Verlaine's "L'Angélus du matin," (*Jadis et naguère*, 1884)—or, more common in Verlaine, as dusk falls—explored in "Crépuscule du soir mystique" (*Poèmes saturniens*, 1866) and "Les Ingénus" (*Fêtes galantes*, 1869). While Verlaine's imagery is ethereal,

Baudelaire's twilight scenes in "Crépuscule du soir" and "Crépuscule du matin" (*Tableaux Parisiens*) dwell on life as lived in the cracks and crevices of urban Paris, thereby serving up an ironic appreciation for the ambiguity between shades of light and dark.

Baudelaire's treatment of the moon was often less idealistic than Verlaine's, as seen in poems from Baudelaire's *Les Fleurs du mal*. In "Le Revenant" the moon takes on a distinctly grotesque aura: "And I will give to my dark mate, cold kisses, frigid as the moon."[13] A taunting moon is again present in "Chanson d'après-midi" (1860): "You wound me, my brunette, with ever-mocking smile, then sweetly, like the moon, gaze on my heart a while."[14] The moon as a harbinger of hard, cold truth is explored in "La lune offensée," where it sees what humans cannot; here, the moon's harsh light exposes the inadequacies of modern life.

Baudelaire's prose poems heighten the macabre tone of his nighttime visions, thereby placing Debussy's musical evocations at somewhat of a distance. At some moments, Baudelaire prolongs the longstanding association of twilight, darkness, and the moon with aspects of human consciousness and the powers of the imagination in keeping with that of the Romantics. In "Le Crépuscule du soir," for instance, the transition to evening is a catalyst for what remains dormant and unseen in broad daylight. "O night," he writes, turning to evening as a source of poetic inspiration, "O refreshing dark! For me you signal inward celebration; you deliver me from anguish."[15] In the same moment, however, Baudelaire associates nighttime with madness, thus anticipating the aesthetic leanings of Symbolist and Decadent writers.

A similar feeling of uneasiness pervades Baudelaire's treatment of the link between the moon and femininity. His poem "Le vin du solitaire" (1857) extends a Romantic image: "A handsome woman's tantalizing gaze gliding our way as softly as the beam the sinuous moon sends out in silver sheen across the lake to bathe her careless rays."[16] His prose poems, however, suggest a more sinister interpretation. Baudelaire underscores the moon's menacing nature in "Le desir de peindre" (1863) through the invocation of opposites. Thus, it is not a white moon that he speaks of but one that is more like a black sun, "sinister and intoxicating, hung in the depth of a stormy night and assaulted by moving clouds." He continues: "Not the peaceable discreet moon visiting the sleep of the pure, but the moon vanquished and rebellious, ripped from the sky."[17] Another prose poem, "Les Bienfaits de la lune" (1863), extends this mood by characterizing the moon as an evil godmother, "a poisonous nurse of all lunatics."[18]

Verlaine responded to both the idealistic and the macabre tones of Baudelaire's nocturnal scenes. Baudelaire associated the moon with dreaming in "Tristesses de la lune" (1850): "When sometimes from her stupefying calm on to this earth she [the moon] drops a furtive tear pale as an opal, iridescent, rare, the poet, sleepless watchman, is the one to take it up within his hollowed palm and in his heart to hide it from the sun."[19] Verlaine also took Baudelaire's characterization of dreaming as truth in "Prologue" (*Jadis et naguère*): "Dim-lit, those visions born of night, of twilight moments just before the dawn: O truth, your pallid light grays them in loathsome shades."[20] The nearest Verlaine came to Baudelaire's tormented visions of the night is also in

"Prologue" (*Jadis et naguère*), where the vanishing light offers an eerie vision of darkness: "The more one looks, the more one wonders whether it is the moonglow that endows those forms with life, coming together beneath the frightening, swaying boughs."[21] Here, the moon is equated with a haunting landscape that gives way to "sunlit harmony." In a late poem, "Réveil," the evening is no longer a facilitator of love and flirting but filled with the portent of death, perhaps indicative of Verlaine's own dismal state toward the end of his life.

Whereas the moon is a source of comfort for the poor poet in Verlaine's "Caprice" (*Parallèlement*, 1889)—"The moon, bringer of warmth to the destitute"—it could also be cold and unwelcoming. Thus, a more sinister tone is felt in "Pierrot" (*Jadis et naguère*), where moonlight accentuates the clown's ghostly appearance. When the moon exudes a supernatural aura in the Faustian "Walpurgisnacht" (*Poèmes saturniens*), it feels Baudelairean: "And there, in response to the horns' call, white shapes suddenly intertwine, translucent, which, amid the green shadow of branches, the moonlight makes opaline—Raffet's dream of Watteau!"[22]

The moon is a constant motif throughout Verlaine's oeuvre, where it serves a variety of literary functions. An early poem, "Marine" (*Poèmes saturniens*), is typically Romantic in its treatment of the moon as the source of a storm and the protagonist from whose perspective we witness the turbulent scene: "The moon, in mourning, eyes the moaning, churning sea."[23] From the same collection, "L'heure du Berger" recalls Baudelaire in its invocation of the tint of a red moon that casts a vermilion shadow over the scene; the poem begins, "The rising moon shines reddish through the mist."[24] Here, the redness of the rising moon invokes the thick red blood into which Baudelaire's sun had previously set: "The sun has drowned in its own congealing blood," ("Harmonie du soir," 1856, set by Debussy in 1889). Echoes of Baudelaire reverberate through Verlaine's "Croquis Parisien" (*Poèmes saturniens*) as well, where the cold moonlight reveals the beauty inherent in urban life: "The moon plated its shades of zinc in blunted angles."[25] Alluding to Baudelaire more explicitly, Verlaine describes a bloody sunset in "Le son du cor s'afflige vers les bois" (*Sagesse*, 1881, set by Debussy in the *Trois mélodies* in 1891). In comparison, the incandescent blue moonlight into which the idle party chatter of Hugo's "La fête chez Thérèse" dissipates seems marvelously dreamy, as it does with its recurrence in Baudelaire's "La mort des amants" (1851), where two lovers bid their final farewells in "an evening that is all mystic blue and pink." Perhaps it is to the collective imagination of Hugo, Baudelaire, and Verlaine that Debussy pays tribute when he exclaims that "nothing is more musical than a sunset!"—a statement that emphasizes the spectacular beauty of music whose transience can only be made permanent through memory and recollection.[26]

Significant for Debussy's Clair de Lune is how Verlaine's treatment of the *fête galante* topic in his "Clair de lune" pays tribute to Baudelaire's "Harmonie du soir" where "the sky is sad and beautiful," a quality Verlaine projects onto the figure of the moon. Verlaine's "Clair de lune" also prolongs the closing mood of his earlier poem, "Le Rossignol" (*Poèmes saturniens*, 1866): "And in the sad splendor of a moon rising pallid and solemn, a heavy melancholy night in summer, full of silence and what is obscure, rocks on the azure a breeze brushes with fingertips the tree that trembles and the bird that weeps."[27] While the moon is calm, sad, and beautiful in Verlaine's "Clair de lune," it is pink and gray in his "Mandoline" (*Fêtes galantes*, set by Debussy in 1882), maybe alluding to the hues of the rich silks in which Watteau's sighing lute player is dressed in his painting *Mezzetin* (1718–1720).

VERLAINE IN ART

Inspired by Watteau's *fêtes galantes*, the erotic and playful undertones of Verlaine's verses as seen in such poems as "Sur l'herbe," "En bateau," and "Fantoches" find an intriguing accompaniment in the post–World War I illustrations of George Barbier (1882–1932). Sketched between 1920 and 1927 and conceived for a limited-edition publication of Verlaine's *Fêtes galantes* in 1928, these illustrations with the clear lines and bold colors of Barbier's art deco style seem far removed from the precious dreamworld of Verlaine's twilight scenes. When viewed as a set, however, each of the twenty hand-colored, luxury pochoir prints captures the essence of Verlaine's poetry through the theatrically trained eye of Barbier. The subtle references to specific paintings by Watteau in these prints reflect not only Barbier's knowledge of Watteau but also his sensitive reading of Verlaine (figure 5.1).

The opening sequence of illustrations takes us into the heart of Verlaine's *Fêtes galantes*. In "Clair de Lune," a magical blue sky—evocative of Hugo but influenced in tone and color by Japanese woodblock prints—forms the backdrop

FIGURE 5.1   George Barbier, *Clair de Lune*, from *Paul Verlaine: Fêtes galantes* (Paris: H. Piazza, 1928). Typ 915.28.8680, Houghton Library, Harvard University.

against which commedia dell'arte personalities mingle among such mythical creatures as the faun and courting aristocrats. In "Pantomime," an open-air theatrical scene features Jean-Gaspard Deburau as Pierrot, followed by a depiction of aristocrats cavorting under a starry sky in "Sur l'herbe." A golden moon emerges gradually in the remaining plates, its first playful placement in "Cortège" forming a delightful instance of trompe l'oeil. Placed low among the clouds, the servant's decorated turban is the same shape and hue of the moon seen in later images of the series, where it appears high in the sky; Barbier is clearly trying to capture the gradual ascent of the moon in this way. In "Fantoches," commedia dell'arte figures are silhouetted against the golden moon on a clear night. The moon peeks through the clouds to witness declarations of love and strains of plucked music in "En bateau" and "En sourdine," while its counterpart, the glistening Pierrot, goes in futile search of love from scene to scene.

The intertextual richness of Barbier's humorous transposition references a variety of visual techniques and artworks, both French and Japanese. As reflected in Barbier's collection, the French admiration for Japanese art, especially woodblock prints in the ukiyo-e style, lasted many years beyond its introduction to French society in the middle of the nineteenth century.[28] The parallels between Barbier's work and such woodblock prints as Utagawa Fusatane's *Summer Scene* (1862), Utagawa Hiroshige's *Nagakubo, The Bridge by Moonlight* (1836), Arai Yoshimune's *Kominato Bay* (ca. 1910–1920), and Koho Shoda's *Lake Biwa* (early twentieth century) are especially strong, reminding us of the degree to which this genre spurred innovation in the French decorative arts well into the twentieth century (figure 5.2).

Barbier's plates are deliberately more action-filled than the tranquil scenes of traditional ukiyo-e and *shin hanga*, the latter representing the more modern form of woodblock design seen with Yoshimune and Shoda. Nonetheless, Barbier's treatment of motif and contrast of color, coupled with the precision of line, directly reference woodblock techniques.

Equally important for Barbier's collection is the work of Félix Vallotton, a Swiss painter, printmaker, and woodcut artist whose first woodcut from 1891 was of Verlaine. Vallotton's attention to Japanese woodblock prints is seen in his decorative treatment of the theme of sunset in a woodcut from 1892, *Le Beau Soir* (figure 5.3). Here, the distinct repeating textures of pebbles and ripples are contrasted against the lonely figure of an elderly man gazing at a still-resplendent sun as it sets behind the hills, his solid placement on the far-right corner being balanced by the haphazard flight of seagulls and rocking boats on the left.

Vallotton's oil painting *Clair de Lune* (1895) builds on the themes of this woodcut while suggesting points of intersection with Barbier's nighttime scenery. The influence of Japanese printmakers is seen in the minimalist, flat landscape and restrained combination of colors in a scene where simplicity of idea is key (figure 5.4). In keeping with Symbolist aesthetics, the decorative figure of the arabesque is given an important function as it sweeps though the landscape in the form of a winding river. Reflected within its subtly winding contour is the lightly golden moon as it peeks through clouds, thereby bringing a little fullness to an otherwise sparse and desolate scene. In addition to the tonal

FIGURE 5.2   Utagawa Fusatane, *Summer scene*. Print, Japan, 1862. © Victoria and Albert Museum, London.

FIGURE 5.3   Félix Vallotton, *Le beau soir* (1892). Woodcut in black on wove
paper, 31.9 cm × 49.3 cm. Van Gogh Museum, Amsterdam.
Artwork in the public domain.

FIGURE 5.4   Félix Vallotton, *Clair de Lune* (1895). Oil on canvas, 27 × 41 cm.
© RMN-Grand Palais/Art Resource, NY.

palette, the decorative features of this scene—the arabesque shape and wavy outline of the clouds—anticipate the outline of Barbier's cloud motifs and shrubbery. With the suggestive silence of Vallotton's painting at one end of the spectrum and the decorative extravagance of Barbier's conception at the other, it seems appropriate to think about what came in between—that is, how the theme of night was transformed in the hands of the Symbolists.

TOWARD A SYMBOLIST MOON

The blood red moon that rises at the end of Poe's short story "The Fall of the House of Usher" suggests a link with Baudelaire's visions of the setting sun. Poe and Baudelaire were both exploring the symbolic potential of such images around the same time, to the extent that when Poe's stories began to appear in French journals around 1841, Baudelaire felt he had discovered a kindred spirit, a revelation that inspired him to translate Poe's writings. It was through these translations that Poe's unique formulation of American gothic horror became an obsession in Paris. Baudelaire's artistic reputation played a role in how quickly his passion for Poe was assimilated by the younger generation, although each artist—including the writers Mallarmé and Paul Valéry, the painters Gustave Moreau and Odilon Redon, and the composers Debussy and Ravel—took from Poe what they needed to buttress their own creative instincts. While French translations of Poe likely helped these Symbolists articulate their aspirations more clearly, Poe's literary exploration of the fantastic, the supernatural, the grotesque, and the arabesque epitomized what many in the French avant-garde aspired to in their collective interest of exploring the realm of sound, sensation, and the subconscious, themes that were synonymous with the night.

The symbolic potential of Poe's favorite objects—the moon, bells, dying women—was eagerly developed across a range of media by European artists. An immediate connection with "Usher" can be sensed in Maeterlinck's play *La Princesse Maleine* (1889), based on the Grimm Brothers' "Maid Maleen." Here, the guards Stephano and Vanox interpret cosmic irregularities as foretelling the tragedy that will befall Maleine. Stephano sees a gigantic comet that "looks like it's spilling blood all over the castle," while Vanox notices how "the moon's turned a strange shade of red."[29] Throughout the drama, the progression of time—and the psychological journey toward death—is marked by changes in weather and time of day. The appearance of the moon in the opening scene tells Vanox and Stephano that it is midnight, while the covering of the moon by clouds anticipates the fateful meeting between Prince Hjalmar and Maleine, something that the Prince also picks up on. "I never saw this autumn wood stranger than it is tonight," he reflects. "I never saw this wood darker than it is tonight. . . . And the way the clouds quiver against the moon!" Queen Anne compares the bewildered (disguised) Maleine to an alien— "Did you drop down from the moon?"—an association that is made real when the moon, otherwise concealed by clouds, shines on the princess at the moment she reveals herself to Prince Hjalmar in the dark woods.[30] The eclipse of the moon in the final act speaks of Maleine's murder. The "eerie" moon, as described by the lords, is interpreted by the peasants as a sign of the Last Judgment.

The eeriness and constant presence of the moon in *La Princesse Maleine* likely influenced Oscar Wilde's writing of the play *Salomé*, published in French in 1891. Given Wilde's association with Walter Pater and John Ruskin, he was already familiar with the Pre-Raphaelite painters' exploration of such themes as silence and mystery. What Maeterlinck and the Parisian Symbolists contributed to Wilde's creative approach during his stay in Paris was a desire to upturn social conventions through attention to themes of the subconscious. A connection between Salomé and Princess Maleine is made in the opening lines, where the beauty of Princess Salomé is juxtaposed with the strangeness of the moon. Described as dead and having a strange look, the moon is compared with "a little princess who wears a yellow veil, and whose feet are of silver."[31] The warm, soft glow of the moon experienced in Hugo and Verlaine is completely transformed in Wilde's Decadent play. The character of the Page observes how the moon "is like a woman who is dead. She moves very slowly." And the eclipse from *La Princesse Maleine* haunts Wilde's landscape, where the moon is covered in clouds: "Oh! How strange the moon looks . . . [like] the hand of a dead woman who is seeking to cover herself with a shroud."[32]

The equation between moonlight and death that haunts *La Princesse Maleine* is front and center in *Salomé*. This association was also detected by Aubrey Beardsley, whose Japanese-inspired illustrations for the 1894 English edition open with *The Woman in the Moon*, a black and white line block illustration of the moon wittily inscribed with Wilde's features (figure 5.5). Veiled by jagged clouds, the moon's peering eyes look askance toward an anxiety-laden male

FIGURE 5.5   Aubrey Beardsley, *The Woman in the Moon* (1894). Line block print on Japanese vellum. © Victoria and Albert Museum, London.

couple, the flowing arabesque lines of the young page's full gown contrasting against the man's nakedness.

Like Maeterlinck's guards, it is the ancillary character of the Page who is the only one to sense the closeness of death. When the Page's counterpart, a young soldier, kills himself in revolt against Salomé's sexual conquest of Jokanaan, the Page exclaims, "Ah! Why did I not hide him from the moon?" The characterization of the moon as a dead woman meets its corollary in a subsequent observation concerning the paleness of the princess. Salomé greets the moon, projecting an idealized image of herself onto it. "How good to see the moon! She is like a little piece of money . . . a little silver flower. The moon is cold and chaste."[33] M. Owen Lee is right to claim that "the moon that presides over the action reflects the mental state . . . of each character in turn," since Salomé projects a similar characterization onto the captive Jokanaan: "He is like an image of silver. I am sure he is chaste as the moon is. He is like a moonbeam, like a shaft of silver."[34] Herod, in his unceasing pursuit of Salomé, projects his own sexual fantasies onto the moon: "She is like a mad woman . . . who is seeking everywhere for lovers. She is naked too. She is quite naked. The clouds are seeking to clothe her nakedness . . . She reels though the clouds like a drunken woman."[35] Herod's lustful comments contrast with those of his wife, whose matter-of-factness is captured in her perception of the moon: "No. The moon is like the moon, that is all." But her later association of the moon with madness—"These men are mad. They have looked too long on the moon"—suggests that her comment is meant to distract Herod and make light of the foreboding statements that surround her: "Ah! Ah! I should like to see that day of which he speaks, when the moon shall become like blood."[36]

While Poe's blood-red moon extends its symbolic presence through Wilde's play, the moon in *Salomé* is not just a symbol but also an agent of narrative development. In other words, observations concerning the changing color of the moon are pivotal to how the plot progresses. The redness of the moon that Herod observes signals the passing of time as well as his descent into sin, the consequence of which he tries to avoid by eliminating the sight of the moon so that he is no longer confronted by his own conscience: "Hide the moon! Hide the stars!"[37] As Poe and Baudelaire had shown to Wilde, the white, cold light of the moon often reveals the harsh truth. After Herod's command, the clouds cover the moon, but at the last moment, the moon shines brightly on Salomé, whose presence Herod can no longer bear. Beardsley's corresponding image, *The Climax*, is especially rich; gripping Jokanaan's severed head, an ecstatic Salomé hovers high in the sky, the whiteness of her gown merging with that of the moon. Like Barbier, Beardsley's use of trompe l'oeil is playful. As directed by Herod, are the bubbles of clouds encroaching upon the moon or, as suggested by the direction of the billowy outline, is the moon emerging from behind the clouds?

One final example into which these earlier manifestations flow is Maeterlinck's play, *Pelléas et Mélisande* (1892). As several of Debussy's biographers have noted, Lugné-Poë's 1893 production of the Belgian Symbolist's drama struck a deep chord with Debussy. Noting Debussy's interests in Poe and the writings of Villiers de l'Isle Adams around this time, Edward Lockspeiser observes that Debussy had begun to sketch musical ideas for a scene from *Pelléas* even before he thought to solicit permission from Maeterlinck to recast his play as opera. Debussy was already familiar with Symbolist ideas by this time, having been in contact with Mallarmé since the early 1890s at least and becoming a part of Mallarmé's inner circle through attendance at the poet's intimate Tuesday evening soirées, where he would have met such luminaries as Whistler and Wilde, among others. Still, there was something about Maeterlinck's play—perhaps the "grey tones and shadows [that] were cast from lighting overhead," as described by Lockspeiser, or the Pre-Raphaelite-inspired costumes—which gave specific form to Debussy's Symbolist leanings during this decade.[38] David Willinger explains how "numinous silences suggestive of the unseeable world beyond, now infiltrated Symbolist dialogue into fully realized performances."[39] In drama, the qualities of silence and nothingness that pervaded Symbolist art and poetry subsumed the spectator through their subtle intensity.

One way we might measure the impact of Debussy's encounter with Maeterlinck's play is through stylistic changes in his approach to evoking nature and the moon. In his Hellenic-inspired compositions, Debussy interpreted nature's mythic dimensions through an overtly sensuous sonic presence, as heard in the *Prélude à l'après-midi d'un faune* (1894) and in his settings of poems from Pierre Louÿs's collection *Les Chansons de Bilitis* in the song cycle *Trois Chansons de Bilitis* (1899). This tendency became even more refined in the *Trois Nocturnes* (1897–1899), an orchestral work possibly derived in part from an earlier project, *Trois scènes au crépuscule*, inspired by Henri de Régnier's *Poèmes anciens et romanesques* (1887–1889). Debussy's opening movement of the *Nocturnes*, Nuages, shows a remarkable sense of restraint in its preoccupation with a few musical motifs whose substance is revealed through subtle and gradual changes in harmony and instrumentation. And the sense of stasis inherent in Debussy's music recalls his earlier desire to "sacrifice dramatic action to an expression of the long exploration of inner feelings" when working on his *Diane au bois*.[40] Together with Mallarmé's interest in capturing "fugitive impressions," the defining features of Maeterlinck's dramatic conception—with its mostly listless characters, overarching lack of motivation, and proclivity for shades of darkness—spoke directly to artists like Mallarmé and Debussy, who had long been searching for a way to capture and prolong transient sensations of light, movement, and sound.[41] More than anything, the ability to render the invisible realm of atmosphere was one that was highly prized at the fin de siècle among avant-garde groups, regardless of the particular movement or movements with which an artist was identified. Thus, Verlaine chased the twilight; Mallarmé, music; and Maeterlinck, shadows.

Maeterlinck's play is entirely about atmosphere, at least to the extent that Debussy struggled to define Mélisande. "I've spent days trying to capture that 'nothing' that Mélisande is made of," he confided to his friend, the composer Ernest Chausson.[42] As if a reincarnation of Maleine, Mélisande is trapped in the cold, dark kingdom of Allemonde. Throughout, Maeterlinck emphasizes her out-of-placeness through juxtaposition of the light and warmth to which she is drawn with the darkness and cold to which the inhabitants of Allemonde have become accustomed. Golaud discovers Mélisande in the bright daylight of the forest, but she is surrounded by darkness in Allemonde, even when it is day. Debussy's characterization of the night and the moon shares a number of continuities with earlier presentations. In keeping with Baudelaire, for instance, moonlight serves to show what one might not want to see. When Mélisande and Pelléas enter a cave in search of her lost ring, a moonbeam frightens Mélisande by revealing three paupers huddled together in the frigid darkness, barely alive. This was one of the first scenes that Debussy endeavored to set, as suggested in a letter of 1895 to his friend Henri Lerolle: "I think you'll like the scene in front of the cave," he wrote. "I tried to capture all the mystery of the night and the silence in which a blade of grass roused from its slumber makes an alarming noise. And then there's the sea nearby, telling its sorrows to the moon and Pelléas and Mélisande a little scared of talking, surrounded by so much mystery."[43] The connection between a mournful sea and the moon recalls Baudelaire's "Tristesses de la lune," Verlaine's "Marine," Mallarmé's "Apparition" (which Debussy had set in 1882), and "Les fleurs" (from his collection, *Du Parnasse Contemporain*). Debussy takes an additional cue from Maeterlinck—and maybe Maeterlinck from Poe—as conveyed through the eeriness of the setting.

The association between moonlight and love is rendered highly ambivalent by playwright and composer alike. Intent on declaring his love to Mélisande, Pelléas urges her to come under the shade of the linden tree so that they can hide from prying eyes, but Mélisande, always craving light, refuses. Their roles are reversed after they declare their love for one another, with Pelléas wanting to move into the light so that he can see how happy they are, while Mélisande prefers to stay in the dark, where she is closer to him and protected against Golaud's prying eyes.

A different type of otherworldliness is seen in Debussy's treatment of the moon in some of the piano music he wrote in an Orientalist vein after *Pelléas*. In the piece Et la lune descend sur le temple qui fut (*Images*, Book 2, 1907), the music appears to retreat from the harsh moon of Allemonde while retaining a link to this ancient, distant realm. Two pianists who were familiar with Debussy's piano music, Alfred Cortot and Marguerite Long, both described this movement using Orientalist imagery.[44] Cortot mused on the title in speaking of "the meditative beauty of a site slowly composed by time, which pursues into the misty night the silent dream of its ruins." Long described the textural novelty of the piece in terms of gongs "in the dead temple," before suggesting a descriptive role for the moon as it descends over temple ruins: "But is it not in the pure style of the art of the Far East to give as much importance to its setting as to the object itself?"[45]

Another piano piece from around this time, La terrasse des audiences du clair de lune (*Preludes*, Book 2, 1913) shows how Debussy's vision of the Orient was often intertwined with his explorations of Frenchness. The title for this piece is believed to have been inspired by a newspaper article by René Puaux about the coronation of King George V as Emperor of India.[46] According to Vallas, Debussy was struck by Puaux's phrase "La salle de la victoire, la salle du plaisir, le jardin du sultanes, la terrasse des audiences au clair de la lune" ("The hall of victory, the hall of pleasure, the garden of the Sultans, the terrace for moonlit audiences").[47] Many scholars of Debussy's music have noted the surreptitious ways in which he quotes his own music. Vallas, for his part, hears Debussy's efforts to establish this moonlit scene through a subtle reference to the French nursery rhyme "Au clair de la lune" in the opening measure, the same melody to which Debussy alluded in one of his first songs to invoke the moon, his setting of Banville's "Pierrot."[48] Debussy transforms the rhythmically simple, major key phrase of the nursery rhyme into an almost unrecognizable variant characterized by metric ambiguity and clothed in a disorienting succession of seventh chords. In this way, Debussy shows the French subject losing a sense of self as their defining qualities are altered through imaginary encounter with a foreign realm.

THE FAIREST OF THEM ALL

A consideration of Debussy's earliest engagement with the *fêtes galantes* through Banville's "Pierrot" takes us back full circle to the discussion with which I opened this chapter. It is also a fitting way to close a book on Debussy's Clair de Lune, since the moon that torments Pierrot in Banville's poem is the same one to which Debussy was partial throughout his life, despite the many other lunar depictions that no doubt shaped his own.

In two articles written during his years as a critic for the Société Internationale de Musique (1912–1914), Debussy continued to dream of Watteau. In "The End of the Year" (January 15, 1913), Debussy reminisced about the great harpsichord composers of the eighteenth century. He described Couperin as "the most poetic of our harpsichordists, whose tender melancholy is like that enchanting echo that emanates from the depths of a Watteau landscape, filled with plaintive figures." This phrase brings to mind several of Watteau's paintings, but especially *La Perspective* (1714–1715), where a sliver of sunlight filters through tall trees as figures huddle beneath in their shadows.[49] A specific association between melancholy and moonlight is made in a later article from February 15, 1913, entitled "Taste." "After the god Pan had put together the seven pipes of the syrinx," Debussy wrote, "he was at first only able to imitate the long, melancholy note of the toad wailing in the moonlight."[50] We might sense the presence of this sad note in Watteau's *Pierrot Content* (1712) where an asymmetric patch of sky gives just enough light to reveal a statue of Pan positioned in the center of the painting (in profile; figure 5.6). Placed deep within the foliage, Pan stands directly behind Pierrot, who gazes straight at the viewer through a characteristically blank yet plaintive stare, almost smiling.

Despite the different manifestations of nocturnal scenes to which Debussy was drawn throughout his career, his unwavering focus on the eighteenth century during his final dismal years is significant. In the face of intestinal cancer and a fragile financial situation, Debussy continued to idealize Couperin, Rameau, and Watteau. These artists accompanied deep reflection on his status as a French composer, while providing a source of much-needed comfort and solace, especially during the years of the First World War. In this sense, Debussy was very much a man of his time, given the fervor with which he fell under the spell of Watteau.

Jean-Antoine Watteau, *Pierrot Content* (ca. 1712). Oil on canvas, 35 × 31 cm. Museo Thyssen-Bornemisza/Scala/Art Resource, NY. Artwork in the public domain.

While much of this chapter has focused on the significance of Hugo, Banville, Gauthier, Baudelaire, Verlaine, and Mallarmé, the paintings of Watteau remain an important source for understanding the emotional nuances of Debussy's work. When the Goncourt brothers identified a trace of "tristesse musicale" running through Watteau's oeuvre, they effectively threw down a gauntlet to poets, painters, and musicians of the time, many of whom responded by striving to capture the painter's "sad musicality" through verse, color, and sound.[51] Despite the many forms in which Clair de Lune exists today, hearing it as a product of this artistic context takes us into the heart of Debussy's milieu, where, thanks to the critical reception of Watteau, French depictions of the moon were first and foremost synonymous with melancholy, dreaming, and the imaginary, topics with which Debussy's Clair de Lune continues to be aligned today.

Even though the chief protagonist of this book is Debussy himself, the reader will no doubt have sensed that the composer has shared this honor with the painter, whose depictions of fountains, statues, parks, music, love, and theater wafted just as readily into Verlaine's poetry as into Debussy's compositions. While the first half of this book takes Debussy as the centerpiece in thinking about issues in reception, cultural transformation, and music history, the second half immerses Debussy's piece in the tradition of the *fêtes galantes*, whose spirit pervades the music and, in so doing, points toward Watteau and Verlaine as the muses for his Clair de Lune and many others of the nineteenth century and beyond.

ADDITIONAL SOURCES
FOR READING AND
LISTENING

A good place to start getting to know the composer's world-view is through his letters as compiled and translated by François Lesure and Roger Nichols in *Debussy Letters* (Faber, 1987). Two other sources that are useful for gaining acquaintance with Debussy's personality and aesthetic outlook include Richard Langham Smith's edited volume *Debussy on Music: The Critical Writings of the Great French Composer* (Cornell University Press, 1988) and Roger Nichols's *Debussy Remembered* (Faber & Faber, 1992).

For a broader historical and cultural understanding of Debussy's place in his milieu, I would suggest Edward Lockspeiser's two-volume work *Debussy: His Life and Mind* (Macmillan, 1962–65). This can be supplemented with recent publications that probe more deeply on topics related to history, culture, aesthetics, performance, and musical style: *Debussy in Performance*, edited by James Briscoe (Yale

University Press, 1999); *Debussy and His World*, edited by Jane Fulcher (Princeton University Press, 2001); *Debussy Studies*, edited by Richard Langham Smith (Cambridge University Press, 2009); and *The Cambridge Companion to Debussy*, edited by Simon Tresize (Cambridge University Press, 2011). For readers who are interested in learning more about Debussy's musical language, I recommend Mark DeVoto's *Debussy and the Veil of Tonality: Essays on His Music* (Pendragon, 2004) and *Rethinking Debussy*, edited by Elliott Antokoletz and Marianne Wheeldon (Oxford University Press, 2011).

Debussy's music is widely recorded and readily available for listening through the usual channels. I would like to draw special attention to the recordings with Debussy himself at the piano, produced by Welte Mignon using the now-antiquated technology of reproducing piano rolls. These recordings were later realized by Kenneth Caswell and are available on the CD *Claude Debussy: The Composer as Pianist* (Pierian Recording Society, 2000). Here, Debussy accompanies Mary Garden and plays some of his solo repertoire for piano.

NOTES

CHAPTER 1

1 See http://www.google.com/doodles/claude-debussys-151st-birthday, accessed October 4, 2017.

2 See *Debussy Letters*, trans. Roger Nichols (Cambridge, MA: Harvard University Press, 1987), 118.

3 George Copeland, "Debussy, the Man I Knew," *Atlantic Monthly*, January 1955, 38.

4 See Robert Orledge, *Debussy and the Theatre* (Cambridge: Cambridge University Press, 2009), 204. Debussy also wrote to Ernest Chausson in 1893 about using silence "as a means of expression and perhaps the only way to underline the emotion of a phrase." See *Claude Debussy: Lettres, 1884–1918*, ed. François Lesure (Paris: Hermann, 1980), 55.

5 See, for instance, Matthew Brown, *Debussy Redux: The Impact of his Music on Popular Culture* (Bloomington: Indiana University Press, 2012); Bernard Gendron, *Between Montmartre and the Mudd Club: Popular Music and the Avant-Garde* (Chicago: University of Chicago Press, 2002); and Michael Long, *Beautiful Monsters: Imagining the Classic in Musical Media* (Berkeley: University of California Press, 2008).

6 *Debussy Letters*, 41.

7 Pierre Lalo, *Le Temps*, October 24, 1905. For Debussy's response to Lalo, see *Debussy Letters*, 163–64.

8 Alfred Cortot, *The Piano Music of Claude Debussy*, trans. Violet Edgell (London: J. & W. Chester, 1922), 9.

9 Peter Dayan, "Nature, Music, and Meaning in Debussy's Writings," *19th-Century Music* 28 (2005): 221.

10 *Debussy on Music: The Critical Writings of the Great French Composer*, ed. and trans. Richard Langham Smith (Ithaca, NY: Cornell University Press, 1988), 199.

11 *Debussy on Music*, 279.

CHAPTER 2

1 See Claude Debussy, *Suite Bergamasque*, ed. Roy Howat (Paris: Durand, 2002).

2 I regret not being able to discuss examples from TV and dance in this chapter. I refer the reader to IMDb for a comprehensive list of instances where Clair de Lune appears in TV and film. An excellent balletic interpretation choreographed by Luke Robson can be viewed on YouTube at https://www.youtube.com/watch?v=LAXU2hVMWMU, accessed October 4, 2017.

3 *Debussy Letters*, trans. Roger Nichols (Cambridge, MA: Harvard University Press, 1987), 190.

4 *Debussy Letters*, 225.

5 Wylna Blanche Hudson, *Musical Courier*, February 12, 1908, 30.

6 James Briscoe, "Debussy in Daleville: Toward Early Modernist Hearing in the United States," in *Rethinking Debussy*, ed. Elliott Antokoletz and Marianne Wheeldon (New York: Oxford University Press, 2011), 238.

7 See Keir Keightley, "Music for Middlebrows: Defining the Easy Listening Era, 1946–1966," *American Music* 26 (2008): 309–35.

8 Pierre Bourdieu, *Distinction: A Social Critique of the Judgement of Taste*, trans. Richard Nice (Cambridge, MA: Harvard University Press, 1984).

9 Rebecca Leydon, "The Soft-Focus Sound: Reverb as a Gendered Attribute in Mid-Century Mood Music," *Perspectives of New Music* 39 (2001): 96–107.

10 Available on YouTube at https://www.youtube.com/watch?v=oluvHgyoxko, accessed October 4, 2017.

11 *Billboard*, October 27, 1956, 54.

12 Leydon, "Soft-Focus Sound," 99.

13 *Billboard Music Week*, July 3, 1961. Available on YouTube at https://www.youtube.com/watch?v=ZwL-mbkajpo, accessed October 4, 2017.

14 Available on YouTube at https://www.youtube.com/watch?v=BRs8P14IZkE, accessed October 4, 2017.

15 Available on YouTube at https://www.youtube.com/watch?v=IwgdwGKK4U8, accessed October 4, 2017.

16 See Matthew Brown, *Debussy Redux: The Impact of his Music on Popular Culture* (Bloomington: Indiana University Press, 2012), 150–51.

17 Available on YouTube at https://www.youtube.com/watch?v=xsi4iiojZT8, accessed October 4, 2017.

18 Claude Debussy, "Monsieur Croche the Dilettante Hater," in *Three Classics in the Aesthetic of Music*, trans. B. N. Langdon Davies (New York: Dover, 1962), 4.

19 Michael Long, *Beautiful Monsters: Imagining the Classic in Musical Media* (Berkeley: University of California Press, 2008), 16.

20 Available on YouTube at https://www.youtube.com/watch?v=osZ749y2dZU, accessed October 4, 2017.

21 See Brown, *Debussy Redux*, 66–79, and https://www.youtube.com/watch?v=sRRk7JChSts, accessed October 4, 2017.

22 Available on YouTube at https://www.youtube.com/watch?v=lKlBTmylvqY, accessed October 4, 2017.

23 Available on YouTube at https://www.youtube.com/watch?v=jq3ol5-vBbo, accessed October 4, 2017.

24 Timothy Taylor, *The Sounds of Capitalism: Advertising, Music, and the Conquest of Culture* (Chicago: University of Chicago Press, 2012), 1, and Nicholas Cook, *Analysing Musical Multimedia* (Oxford: Clarendon, 1998), 3–23.

25 Available on YouTube at https://www.ispot.tv/ad/7JJA/mcdonalds-ingredients, accessed October 4, 2017.

26 Available on YouTube at https://www.youtube.com/watch?v=536L-IdpXgo, accessed October 4, 2017.

27 See Pam Cook, *Baz Luhrmann* (London: Palgrave Macmillan, 2010), 32.

28 Available on YouTube at https://www.youtube.com/watch?v=nfoMbir_Qd4, accessed October 4, 2017.

29 See Léon Vallas, *Claude Debussy: His Life and Works*, trans. Maire O'Brien and Grace O'Brien (New York: Dover, 1973), 4, and John R. Clevenger, "Debussy's Paris Conservatoire Training," in *Debussy's World*, ed. Jane Fulcher (Princeton, NJ: Princeton University Press, 2001), 299–361.

30 *Debussy on Music: The Critical Writings of the Great French Composer*, ed. and trans. Richard Langham Smith (Ithaca, NY: Cornell University Press, 1988), 295.

31 Vallas, *Claude Debussy*, 85.

32 Louise Liebich, *Claude-Achille Debussy* (John Lane: London, 1908), 25; John House, *Monet: Nature into Art* (New Haven, CT: Yale University Press, 1986), 221.

33 *Debussy on Music*, 48.

34 House, *Monet: Nature into Art*, 221.

35 *Debussy Letters*, 188.

36 Henri Dorra, ed., *Symbolist Art Theories: A Critical Anthology* (Berkeley: University of California Press, 1995), 141.

37 Vallas, *Claude Debussy*, 84; translation modified slightly.

38 See http://www.imdb.com/name/nm0006033/, accessed October 4, 2017.

39 Robynn J. Stilwell, "The Fantastical Gap between Diegetic and Nondiegetic," in *Beyond the Soundtrack: Representing Music in Cinema*, ed. Daniel Goldmark,

Lawrence Kramer, and Richard Leppert (Berkeley: University of California Press, 2007), 186.

40 See, for instance, "Phonoplay: Recasting Film Music," in Goldmark, Kramer, and Leppert, *Beyond the Soundtrack*, 3.

41 Jeremy Barham, "Recurring Dreams and Moving Images: The Cinematic Appropriation of Schumann's Op. 15, No. 7," *19th-Century Music* 34 (2011): 299.

42 See Rick Altman, *Silent Film Sound* (New York: Columbia University Press, 2004), 315–17.

43 Available on YouTube at https://www.youtube.com/watch?v=FcpamvLB2JU, accessed October 4, 2017.

44 Robin Allan, *Walt Disney and Europe: European Influences on the Animated Feature Films of Walt Disney* (Bloomington: Indiana University Press, 1999), 263.

45 For an excellent study of *Fantasia* and its relationship to American culture of the 1940s, see Mark Clague, "Playing in 'Toon: Walt Disney's *Fantasia* (1940) and the Imagineering of Classical Music," *American Music* 22 (2004): 91–109.

46 See Annegret Fauser, "Sounding the *Tricolore*: France and the United States during World War II," *Les Cahiers de la Société québécoise de recherche en musique* 16 (2017): 13.

47 Available on YouTube at https://www.youtube.com/watch?v=seTNZnddggs, accessed October 4, 2017.

48 Charles Higham, *Kate: The Life of Katharine Hepburn* (New York: W. W. Norton, 1975), 127.

49 Available on YouTube at https://www.youtube.com/watch?v=t9SkNLboE1o, accessed October 4, 2017.

50 Stephenie Meyer, *Twilight* (New York: Little, Brown, 2005), 104–5.

51 The *Los Angeles Times* reports an interview with the Dalai Lama where he speaks of "a fascination with a music box that played Debussy's 'Clair de Lune.'" See Mark Swed, "The Dalai Lama's View," *Los Angeles Times*, September 19, 1999; available online at http://articles.latimes.com/1999/sep/19/entertainment/ca-11719/2, accessed October 4, 2017.

52 Ian McEwan, *Atonement: A Novel* (New York: Anchor, 2003), 290.

53 Cheryl Ganz, *The 1933 Chicago World's Fair: A Century of Progress* (Urbana: University of Illinois Press, 2012), 7–27.

54 Available on YouTube at https://www.youtube.com/watch?v=SRSbYXutreE, accessed October 4, 2017.

55 For a detailed study of Clair de Lune in *Ocean's Eleven*, see Brent A. Ferguson, "Moonlight in Movies: An Analytical Interpretation of Claude Debussy's 'Clair de Lune' in Selected American Films" (master's thesis, Texas State University at San Marcos, 2011), 57–74.

56 Available on YouTube at https://www.youtube.com/watch?v=Cfu9s89C-pc, accessed October 4, 2017.

57 Phil Savage, "The Evil Within Trailer Features Classical Music, Long Walks," *PC Gamer*, September 17, 2014, available online at http://www.pcgamer.com/the-evil-within-trailer-features-classical-music-long-walks/, accessed October 4, 2017.

58 Gregor Herzfeld, "Atmospheres at Play: Aesthetical Considerations of Game Music," in *Music and Game Perspectives on a Popular Alliance*, ed. Peter Moorman (Wiesbaden, Germany: Springer, 2013), 148.

59 See Christopher, "Upcoming Game, RAIN, Features Debussy's Clair de Lune," *Tracksounds* (blog), March 26, 2013, http://blog.tracksounds.com/2013/03/upcoming-game-rain-features-debussys.html, accessed October 4, 2017.

60 See fan comments on Metacritic at http://www.metacritic.com/game/playstation-3/rain, accessed October 4, 2017. For critics' comments see http://www.metacritic.com/game/playstation-3/rain/critic-reviews, accessed October 4, 2017), and Daniel Krupa, "Rain Review," *IGN*, October 1, 2013, http://www.ign.com/articles/2013/10/01/rain-review, accessed October 4, 2017.

61 See the video "The Music of *Rain*" at http://www.ign.com/articles/2013/10/01/rain-review, accessed October 4, 2017.

62 See Kristina Iwata-Weickgennant and Roman Rosenbaum, eds., *Visions of Precarity in Japanese Popular Culture and Literature* (New York: Routledge, 2015), 117–31.

63 Available on YouTube at https://www.youtube.com/watch?v=aKiBnRMMfpU, accessed October 4, 2017.

64 See Dan Stapleton, "ADRiFT Review," *IGN*, March 28, 2016, http://www.ign.com/articles/2016/03/28/adrift-review, accessed October 4, 2017); Justin McElroy, "Adrift Review," *Polygon*, March 31, 2016, http://www.polygon.com/2016/3/31/11334468/adrift-review-adrift-pc-oculus-rift-vr, accessed October 4, 2017); and Kyle Orland, "*Adrift* Review: It's Lonely Out in Space," *Ars Technica*, March 28, 2016, http://arstechnica.com/gaming/2016/03/adrift-review-its-lonely-out-in-space-embargo-10am-monday-328/, accessed October 4, 2017.

65 *Debussy Letters*, 246.

66 Ryan J. Stark, "Clichés and Composition Theory," *JAC* 19, no. 3 (1999): 453.

67 See Gary A. Olson, "The Generational Cliché: Then You Saw It; Now They Don't," *Journal of Advanced Composition* 6 (1985–86): 114.

68 Stark, "Clichés and Composition Theory," 454.

CHAPTER 3

1 See Roy Howat, *The Art of French Piano Music: Debussy, Ravel, Fauré, Chabrier* (New Haven, CT: Yale University Press, 2009), and Robert Orledge, "Debussy's Piano Music: Some Second Thoughts and Sources of Inspiration," *Musical Times* 122 (1981): 21–27.

2 Robert Orledge, *Debussy and the Theatre* (Cambridge: Cambridge University Press, 2009), 152.

3 Robert Orledge, *Gabriel Fauré* (London: Eulenberg, 1979), 191.

4 Verlaine, "Clair de Lune."

5 Verlaine, "Clair de Lune."

6 Vladimir Jankélévitch, *Music and the Ineffable*, trans. Carolyn Abbate (Princeton, NJ: Princeton University Press, 2003), 111.

7 Jankélévitch, *Music and the Ineffable*, 82.

CHAPTER 4

1 Maxine Cutler, *Evocations of the Eighteenth Century in French Poetry, 1800–1869* (Geneva: Droz, 1970), 196.

2 Judy Sund explores this revival in more detail in "Why So Sad? Watteau's Pierrots," *Art Bulletin* 98 (2016): 333.

3 Guillaume Faroult, "Watteau and Chardin, 'The Two Most Truly *Painters* of the Entire French School': The Rediscovery of Watteau and Chardin in France between 1820 and 1860," in *Delicious Decadence: The Rediscovery of French Eighteenth-Century Painting in the Nineteenth Century*, ed. Guillaume Faroult, Monica Preti, and Christoph Vogtherr (Burlington, VT: Ashgate, 2014), 36.

4 Their essay "La Philosophie de Watteau" was first published on September 7, 1856, in the journal *L'Artiste*.

5 Edmond and Jules de Goncourt, *L'art du dix-huitième siècle* (Paris: Charpentier, 1902), 1:11.

6 For example, Camille Benoit transformed the Goncourts' phrase in speaking of the "delicious sadness" of Fauré's Requiem, a piece he described in comparison with *L'Embarquement pour Cythère*; see his "La Messe de Requiem," *Le Guide Musical*, August 9 and 16, 1888, 196–97. Jean d'Udine (pseudonym of Albert Cozanet) compared Fauré's song "Clair de Lune" with the same painting in his *Paraphrases Musicales sur les grands concerts du dimanche (Colonne et Lamoureux), 1900–1903* (Paris: A. Joanin, 1904), 203.

7 See Robert Orledge, *Gabriel Fauré* (London: Eulenberg, 1979), 191.

8 As discussed by Cutler, Théodore de Banville, Emmanuel des Essarts, and Théophile Gautier were among those who had paid homage to Watteau in several of their poems before Verlaine; see Cutler, *Evocations of the Eighteenth Century*, 209–11. There are numerous other examples, such as the chapter "Voyage to Cythera" in Gérard de Nerval's novella *Sylvie* (1853) and Charles Baudelaire's "Un Voyage à Cythère" (*Les Fleurs du Mal*).

9 Jacques-Henry Bornecque explains that following Anatole France's criticism, Verlaine changed the line as well as the title of the poem, which was "Fêtes

Galantes" when it was first published in *La Gazette rimée*. See Bornecque, *Lumières sur les Fêtes Galantes de Paul Verlaine* (Paris: Nizet, 1959), 148–53.

10 Alfred E. Carter, *Verlaine: A Study in Parallels* (Toronto: University of Toronto Press, 1969), 44; Cutler, *Evocations of the Eighteenth Century*, 237.

11 As cited in Gurminder K. Bhogal, *Details of Consequence: Ornament, Music and Art in French Music* (New York: Oxford University Press, 2013), 188.

12 Pamela Whedon, "Sensing Watteau: The Artist's Musical Images as Preludes to the Age of Sensibility," (PhD diss., University of Carolina at Chapel Hill, 2008), 168.

13 Pierre Rosenberg, "The Paintings," in *Watteau: 1684–1721*, ed. Margaret Morgan Grasselli and Pierre Rosenberg (Washington, DC: National Gallery of Art, 1984), 278.

14 Ken Ireland, *Cythera Regained?: The Rococo Revival in European Literature and the Arts, 1830–1910* (Madison, NJ: Fairleigh Dickinson University Press, 2006), 31; Rosenberg, "Paintings," 434; Martin Green and John Swan, *The Triumph of Pierrot: The Commedia dell'Arte and the Modern Imagination* (University Park: Pennsylvania State University Press, 1993), 4.

15 Edward Nye, "The Romantic Myth of Jean-Gaspard Deburau," *Nineteenth-Century French Studies* 44 (2015–16): 48.

16 Théodore de Banville, *Oeuvres de Théodore de Banville: Odes Funambulesques* (Paris: Librairie Alphonse Lemerre, 1873), 129.

17 See Bornecque, *Lumières sur les Fêtes Galantes*, 149–50.

18 Roger Nichols, "Debussy's Two Settings of 'Clair de lune,'" *Music and Letters* 48 (1967): 230.

19 In keeping with Nichols, Alfred Wright also notes how "Debussy . . . in his more mature settings, sought to frame or support the poem with music which explains or reinforces the changing sentiments of the text—a very supple, expressive music, more closely allied to the individual phrases of the poem than Fauré's." See "Verlaine and Debussy: Fêtes galantes," *French Review* 40 (1967): 628.

20 Available on YouTube at https://www.youtube.com/watch?v=4zHDg3Eo9XU, accessed October 4, 2017.

21 Available on YouTube at https://www.youtube.com/watch?v=uA5FwKzoieg, accessed October 4, 2017.

22 Léon Vallas, *Claude Debussy: His Life and Works*, trans. Maire O'Brien and Grace O'Brien (New York: Dover, 1973), 74.

23 Goncourt, *L'art du dix-huitième siècle*, 5.

24 Vladimir Jankélévitch, *Gabriel Fauré et ses mélodies* (Paris: Librairie Plon, 1951), 93.

25 Graham Johnson and Richard Stokes, *A French Song Companion* (New York: Oxford University Press, 2000), 165.

26 In keeping with the *fêtes galantes* mood of the *Petite Suite*, Mark DeVoto mentions that musical material of Debussy's song "Fête galante" (1882) was reworked as the Menuet of the *Petite Suite*. See his *Debussy and the Veil of Tonality: Essays on his Music* (Hillsdale, NY: Pendragon, 2004), 20.

27 Maurice Dumesnil, "Coaching with Debussy," *Piano Teacher* 5 (1962): 11.

28 Jean-Jacques Eigeldinger, "Chopin and 'La Note Bleue': An Interpretation of the Prelude Op. 45," *Music and Letters* 78 (1997): 240.

29 For a detailed discussion of the arabesque, see Bhogal, *Details of Consequence*.

30 Dumesnil, "Coaching with Debussy," 11.

31 Roy Howat, "Debussy's Piano Music: Sources and Performance," in *Debussy Studies*, ed. Richard Langham Smith (Cambridge: Cambridge University Press, 1997), 102.

32 See Roy Howat, *The Art of French Piano Music: Debussy, Ravel, Fauré, Chabrier* (New Haven, CT: Yale University Press, 2009), 247.

33 Dumesnil, "Coaching with Debussy," 11.

34 Dumesnil, "Coaching with Debussy," 11. Moiseiwitsch's recording is available on YouTube at https://www.youtube.com/watch?v=H5-LD1sAK8g, accessed October 4, 2017.

35 Available on YouTube at https://www.youtube.com/watch?v=ZtN_Iyq7s6M, accessed October 4, 2017.

36 Available on YouTube at https://www.youtube.com/watch?v=XBweTHrOwEU, accessed October 4, 2017.

37 Roger Nichols, *Debussy Remembered* (London: Faber & Faber, 1992), 183.

38 Deborah Priest, *Louis Laloy (1874–1944) on Debussy, Ravel and Stravinsky* (Aldershot, UK: Ashgate, 1999), 107.

39 *Debussy Letters*, trans. Roger Nichols (Cambridge, MA: Harvard University Press, 1987), 274.

40 Priest, *Louis Laloy*, 108.

41 Priest, *Louis Laloy*, 109; Howat, *Art of French Piano Music*, 307; Dumesnil, "Coaching with Debussy," 11.

42 Nichols, *Debussy Remembered*, 202, 55.

43 Dumesnil, "Coaching with Debussy," 11.

44 Nichols, *Debussy Remembered*, 4.

45 Nichols, *Debussy Remembered*, 50.

46 Nichols, *Debussy Remembered*, 72.

47 Déirdre Donnellon, "Debussy, Satie and the Parisian Critical Press (1890–1925)," (PhD diss., University of Liverpool, January 2000), 319.

48 See Cecilia Dunoyer, "Debussy and Early Debussystes at the Piano," in *Debussy in Performance*, ed. James Briscoe (New Haven, CT: Yale University Press, 1999), 105, 113.

49 I am grateful to Rick Masters for sharing an early recording made by Copeland.

CHAPTER 5

1 Quoted in Léon Vallas, *Claude Debussy: His Life and Works*, trans. Maire O'Brien and Grace O'Brien (New York: Dover, 1973), 53.

2 See, for instance, Stefan Jarociński, *Debussy: Impressionism and Symbolism*, trans. Rollo Myers (London: Eulenberg, 1976), and Marie Rolf, "Symbolism as Compositional Agent in Act IV, Scene 4 of Debussy's Pelléas et Mélisande," in *Berlioz and Debussy: Sources, Contexts and Legacies—Essays in Honour of François Lesure*, ed. Barbara Kelly and Kerry Murphy (Aldershot, UK: Ashgate, 2007), 117–48.

3 Barbara Miller's translation captures the satirical flavor of Musset's poem. It is available online at the LiederNet Archive, http://www.lieder.net/lieder/get_text.html?TextId=25387, accessed October 4, 2017.

4 Available on YouTube at https://www.youtube.com/watch?v=VpDl3F7KbKk, accessed October 4, 2017.

5 *The Poetic Debussy: A Collection of His Song Texts and Selected Letters*, ed. Margaret Cobb, trans. Richard Miller (Rochester, NY: University of Rochester Press, 1994), 46–47.

6 Available on YouTube at https://www.youtube.com/watch?v=g2rAxqDsNJg, accessed October 4, 2017.

7 Arthur Wenk, *Claude Debussy and the Poets* (Berkeley: University of California Press, 1976), 317.

8 Wenk, *Claude Debussy*, 312.

9 Philip Stephan, "Verlaine and Baudelaire: Two Uses of Obscured Lightings," *French Review* 35 (1961): 26.

10 James Huneker, *The Poems and Prose Poems of Charles Baudelaire* (New York: Brentano, 1919), xxxv.

11 Stephan, "Verlaine and Baudelaire," 33–34.

12 Charles Baudelaire, *The Flowers of Evil*, trans. James McGowan (New York: Oxford University Press, 1993), 167.

13 Baudelaire, *Flowers of Evil*, 131.

14 Baudelaire, *Flowers of Evil*, 123.

15 Charles Baudelaire, *Paris Spleen: Charles Baudelaire, Little Poems in Prose*, trans. Keith Waldrop (Middletown, CT: Wesleyan University Press, 2009), 44.

16 Baudelaire, *Flowers of Evil*, 223.

17 Baudelaire, *Paris Spleen*, 75.

18 Baudelaire, *Paris Spleen*, 76.

19 Baudelaire, *Flowers of Evil*, 133.

20 Paul Verlaine, *One Hundred and One Poems by Paul Verlaine*, ed. and trans. Norman Shapiro (Chicago: University of Chicago Press, 1999), 137.

21 Verlaine, *One Hundred and One Poems*, 137.

22 Paul Verlaine, *Poems under Saturn / Poèmes saturniens*, trans. Karl Kirchwey (Princeton, NJ: Princeton University Press, 2011), 57.

23 Verlaine, *One Hundred and One Poems*, 7.

24 Verlaine, *One Hundred and One Poems*, 19.

25 Paul Verlaine, *Poems under Saturn*, 35.

26 *Debussy on Music: The Critical Writings of the Great French Composer*, ed. Richard Langham Smith (Ithaca, NY: Cornell University Press, 1988), 199.

27 Verlaine, *Poems under Saturn*, 65.

28 For additional information about Japanese ukiyo-e and its influence on French art of the late nineteenth and early twentieth centuries, see Chelsea Foxwell and Anne Leonard, eds., *Awash in Color: French and Japanese Prints* (Chicago: Smart Museum of Art, 2012).

29 *A Maeterlinck Reader: Plays, Poems, Short Fiction, Aphorisms, and Essays*, ed. and trans. David Willinger and Daniel Gerould (New York: Peter Lang, 2011), 58, 60.

30 *Maeterlinck Reader*, 83, 81.

31 Oscar Wilde, *Salome* (London: John Lane, 1912), 1.

32 Wilde, *Salome*, 2, 19.

33 Wilde, *Salome*, 29, 12–13.

34 See M. Owen Lee, *A Season of Opera: From Orpheus to Ariadne* (Toronto: University of Toronto Press, 1998), 148, and Wilde, *Salome*, 22–23.

35 Wilde, *Salome*, 33.

36 Wilde, *Salome*, 33, 48, 53.

37 Wilde, *Salome*, 81.

38 Edward Lockspeiser, *Debussy: His Life and Mind*, (New York: Macmillan, 1962), 1:190.

39 See David Willinger, "A Life in Counterpoint to a Work," in *A Maeterlinck Reader*, 25.

40 Lockspeiser, *Debussy*, 1:152.

41 Lockspeiser, *Debussy*, 1:152.

42 *Debussy Letters*, trans. Roger Nichols (Cambridge, MA: Harvard University Press, 1987), 62.

43 *Debussy Letters*, 80.

44 Robert Orledge argues that the original title of this piece speaks to Debussy's Orientalist vision: "Et le lune descend sur le temple de Bouddha." See Orledge, "Debussy's Piano Music: Some Second Thoughts and Sources of Inspiration," *Musical Times* 122 (1981): 23. See also Roy Howat, *The Art of French Piano Music: Debussy, Ravel, Fauré, Chabrier* (New Haven, CT: Yale University Press, 2009), 116.

45 Alfred Cortot, *The Piano Music of Claude Debussy*, trans. Violet Edgell (London: J. & W. Chester, 1922), 12; Marguerite Long, *At the Piano with Debussy*, trans. Olive Senior-Ellis (London: Dent, 1972), 81.

46 See Vallas, *Claude Debussy*, 209.

47 Vallas, *Claude Debussy*, 209.

48 Vallas, *Claude Debussy*, 209.

49 *Debussy on Music*, 273.

50 *Debussy on Music*, 279.

51 Edmond and Jules de Goncourt, "La Philosophie de Watteau," *L'Artiste*, September 7, 1856, 127–29.

INDEX